W9-CDH-359

easymediterranean

easy mediterranean

simple recipes from sunny shores

RYLAND
PETERS
& SMALL

LONDON NEW YORK

Senior Designer Paul Tilby
Editor Rachel Lawrence
Production Gemma Moules
Picture Research Emily Westlake
Publishing Director Alison Starling

Index Hilary Bird

First published in the USA in 2007
by Ryland Peters & Small, Inc.
519 Broadway, 5th Floor
New York, NY 10012
www.rylandpeters.com

10 9 8 7 6 5 4 3 2 1

Text © Maxine Clark, Clare Ferguson, Silvana
Franco, Brian Glover, Elsa Petersen-
Schepelern, Louise Pickford, Rena Salaman,
Jennie Shapter, Sonia Stevenson, Linda Tubby,
Fran Warde, and Ryland Peters & Small 2007
Design and photographs
© Ryland Peters & Small 2007

Printed in China

The authors' moral rights have been asserted.
All rights reserved. No part of this publication
may be reproduced, stored in a retrieval
system, or transmitted in any form or by any
means, electronic, mechanical, photocopying,
or otherwise, without the prior permission of
the publisher.

ISBN-10: 1 84597 377 1
ISBN-13: 978 1 84597 377 3

Library of Congress Cataloging-in-Publication Data

Easy Mediterranean simple recipes from sunny
shores / edited by Maxine Clark ... [et al.].
    p. cm.
  Includes index.
  ISBN-13: 978-1-84597-377-3
  1. Cookery, Mediterranean. I. Clark, Maxine,
1955-
  TX725.M35E37 2007
  641.5'91822–dc22

2006030865

Notes

All spoon measurements are level unless
otherwise specified.

Ovens should be preheated to the specified
temperature. If using a convection oven,
cooking times should be reduced according
to the manufacturer's instructions.

Uncooked or partly cooked eggs should not
be served to the very young, the very old or
frail, or to pregnant women.

Specialty Asian ingredients are available in
larger supermarkets and Asian stores.

To sterilize preserving jars, wash them in hot,
soapy water and rinse in boiling water. Place
in a large saucepan and then cover with hot
water. With the saucepan lid on, bring the
water to a boil and continue boiling for
15 minutes. Turn off the heat, then leave the
jars in the hot water until just before they are
to be filled. Sterilize the lids for 5 minutes, by
boiling, or according to the manufacturer's
instructions. Jars should be filled and sealed
while they are still hot.

contents

mediterranean flavors

Famous for its sunshine, sandy shores, and deep blue sea, the Mediterranean is also home to some of the most rich and varied cuisines in the world. From the seafood stews of southern France to the grilled meats of Greece and Turkey, every region has its own distinct dishes and ways of cooking.

Mediterranean cooking centers around exquisite fish and seafood, high-quality meats, and a wealth of fruit, vegetables, pulses, and grains. Thanks to the quality of the ingredients, many dishes are surprisingly easy to make—it's hard to beat a simple pasta dish made with the finest olive oil, juicy vine tomatoes, and fragrant basil, for example. What's more, with its low saturated fat content and emphasis on fresh ingredients, it's healthy, too.

Food culture in this part of the world reflects the relaxed way of life that many Mediterraneans enjoy. Food and drink are things to be savored. The tapas dishes of Spain and meze platters of Greece and Lebanon are classic examples of delicious little morsels designed to be enjoyed at a leisurely pace. At meal times, dishes are often served as separate courses, so that their flavors can be truly appreciated.

Whether you're planning on making a light lunch or a sumptuous feast, this book is packed with ideas and inspiration. With everything from appetizers and snacks to sweet things and drinks, there is something for everyone, including plenty of vegetarian options. So why not bring some sunshine into your kitchen and enjoy the flavors, aromas, and colors of these mouthwatering recipes.

appetizers and snacks

chickpea fritters

Common in Sicily and North Africa, this ancient recipe is a marvelous, easy snack which can also be served with meat or fish. First it is cooked to a sort of thin porridge, which sets. Then it is cut up and cooked a second time, in olive oil, to a sweet crispness. A warning though—do not be tempted to change the order or you will find the mixture becomes lumpy and hard to manage. The fritters also make useful bases for canapés or as "crisps" to serve with creamy dips.

Sieve the chickpea flour and salt together into a heavy-based saucepan. Beat in 2 cups cold water until frothy and lump-free, then stir in the parsley. Bring to a boil, whisking constantly. About 2 minutes after it reaches a boil, it will suddenly thicken—take care as it may splatter.

Keep whisking over the heat for 1 more minute, then pour it out quickly into the oiled tray. Quickly smooth it flat with a spatula to just under ½-inch thickness before it begins to set, about 5–10 minutes.

Mark out into 12 squares, then make diagonal lines to give 24 triangles.

Put the olive oil in a skillet or heavy-based saucepan and heat to 375°F. Add 6–8 triangles at a time and cook for 2 minutes on each side or until golden, blistered, and crisp. Drain on crumpled paper towels. Serve hot or warm.

*Note Chickpea flour, also known as besan or gram flour, is sold in health food outlets, gourmet stores, and Indian grocers.

1¾ cups chickpea flour*

1 teaspoon sea salt

a small bunch of fresh flatleaf parsley, chopped (about ½ cup)

1 cup extra virgin olive oil or olive oil, for frying

a metal tray, about 12 x 16 inches, oiled

MAKES 24

moroccan-style marinated black olives

3 cups black olives in brine

2 tablespoons fennel or cumin seeds, crushed

1 tablespoon green cardamom pods, crushed

1 tablespoon small, hot, dried red chilies

2 tablespoons allspice berries, crushed

3–4 cups extra virgin olive oil

8-inch strip of orange peel, bruised

12 fresh bay leaves, washed, dried, and bruised

1 large jar, 6 cups, sterilized, or 3 jars, 2 cups each

MAKES 6–7 CUPS

Black olives, which have already been cured, will mellow even more if you crack them a little or prick with a fork, then marinate in aromatics and fine olive oil. Experiment, as many Moroccan householders do, until you find a flavor you like—your own customized blend.

Rinse the olives in cold water, drain, then pat dry with paper towels.

Put them on a clean dry surface such as a chopping board and crush them slightly with a meat hammer or rolling pin, or prick with a fork, to open up the flesh a little.

Put the fennel seeds, cardamom, chilies, and allspice berries in a dry skillet and toast over medium heat for a few minutes until aromatic.

Put the olive oil in a saucepan and heat to 350°F—a cube of bread should turn golden-brown in 40–50 seconds. Let cool a little. Using a sterilized spoon, pack the orange peel, bay leaves, olives, and spices into the jar in layers, until they all have been used. Cover with the hot olive oil. Let cool, uncovered. When cold, seal and store in a cool, dark place.

Leave for at least 1 week before tasting. These olives keep well and improve for some months.

This spicy Middle Eastern chickpea dip is deceptively easy to make. Dried chickpeas give a slightly nuttier flavour, but you can use canned chickpeas if you're in a hurry. It is delicious served as a dip with toasted pita breads or Chickpea Fritters (page 10). It also makes a great accompaniment to Falafels (page 20), kabobs, or grilled chicken or meat.

hoummus

1 cup dried chickpeas, soaked in cold water overnight, or one 28-oz. can chickpeas

2 tablespoons tahini paste

2 garlic cloves, chopped

freshly squeezed juice of 1–2 lemons

1 tablespoon ground cumin

2 tablespoons extra virgin olive oil

⅓ cup chickpea cooking liquid

sea salt and freshly ground black pepper

TO SERVE

1 tablespoon extra virgin olive oil

1 tablespoon cilantro, finely chopped

pita bread or triangles of toasted bread

SERVES 6

Drain and rinse the soaked chickpeas and put them in a saucepan. Cover with plenty of water, bring to a boil, and skim until clear. Cover and cook until perfectly soft, about 1 hour. Alternatively, use a pressure cooker, following the manufacturer's instructions—cooking will take about 20 minutes.

Strain the chickpeas, reserving the cooking liquid. If using canned chickpeas, strain them first and discard the liquid, but use about 4 tablespoons cold water in the food processor.

If the tahini paste appears separated in the jar, mix it properly first. Divide all the ingredients into 2 batches and put the first batch in a food processor, then process briefly. Ideally it should still have some texture and should not be too solid. Taste and adjust the seasoning with salt and pepper and blend again briefly. Transfer to a bowl and repeat with the remaining ingredients.

Trickle a little oil over the top and sprinkle with the cilantro. Serve at room temperature with pita bread or triangles of toasted bread. In the summer, it is better served lightly chilled.

Eggplants are a key ingredient in many Mediterranean countries and can be cooked in a variety of ways. Some Middle Eastern cooks barbecue them to make babaghannouj, but in this recipe they are simply cut into cubes, coated in oil, and roasted in the oven, which brings equally good results. This creamy dip can be served warm, cool, or chilled as an appetizer or as part of a mixed meze.

babaghannouj

Toss the cubed eggplants in half the olive oil until coated. Arrange in a single layer in a shallow roasting pan or baking sheet and cook in a preheated oven at 400°F for 20–25 minutes or until tender and slightly frizzled. Put the eggplant and its oil, the remaining olive oil, lemon juice, tahini paste, garlic, parsley and sea salt in a food processor. Blend for about 35–45 seconds to give a coarse but creamy paste. Taste and adjust the seasoning.

Serve warm, cool, or chilled with an optional swirl of yogurt or olive oil on top. Accompany with hot flatbreads or crisp fresh salad leaves.

*Note Tahina, tahine, tahini are variant spellings of the same thing. Though low-fat or less-toasted varieties do exist, you should avoid these. Always go for the full-flavored type.

2 medium eggplants, about 1½ lb., cut into 1-inch cubes

½ cup extra virgin olive oil

¼ cup freshly squeezed lemon juice

¼ cup tahini paste*

3–4 garlic cloves, crushed

a bunch of fresh parsley, chopped

1 teaspoon sea salt flakes

plain yogurt, to taste (optional)

flatbreads or salad greens, to serve

SERVES 4–8

1 cup whole shelled hazelnuts

⅔ cup whole shelled almonds

⅔ cup sesame seeds

½ cup coriander seeds

½ cup ground cumin

1 teaspoon sea salt

½ teaspoon freshly ground black pepper

TO SERVE

extra virgin olive oil

grissini or strips of toasted flatbread

MAKES ABOUT 3½ CUPS

No Egyptian home is complete without a jar of this wonderful seed and nut mixture in the pantry. It is normally eaten as a snack— flatbreads are dipped first into olive oil, then into the dukkah. Grissini work well, too. Dukkah is also great used as a coating for chicken or fish instead of bread crumbs.

egyptian dukkah

Put the hazelnuts, almonds, and sesame seeds in an ovenproof dish in a preheated oven at 400°F and toast for 5–10 minutes. Remove from the oven, then tip onto a plate to cool completely. If they aren't cool enough, they will turn oily when ground.

Toast the coriander seeds in a dry skillet for 1–2 minutes until you can smell the aroma, tip onto the cooling nuts, then add the ground cumin to the pan. Toast for 30 seconds then transfer to the plate. When cold, put the nuts, spices, salt, and pepper in a food processor and blend to a coarse, powdery meal—still dry-looking, but not totally pulverized. Spoon into a bowl and serve on a tray with a bowl of olive oil and the grissini.

falafels

These tasty fava bean patties are packed with fragrant herbs and spices. Falafels are a typical Lebanese street snack often served in pita breads with salad. They can also be served as an appetizer with dips such as Hoummus (page 14), or as part of a more substantial meal with plain rice and a large bowl of refreshing Orange, Frisée, and Black Olive Salad (page 62) or Greek Salad (page 66).

Drain and rinse the beans. Put them in a food processor, then add the onion, garlic, cumin, ground coriander, allspice, cayenne pepper, and baking powder. Process to an almost-smooth paste.

Add the parsley and cilantro and process briefly again. (You may have to divide the ingredients in half and process in 2 batches, depending on the size of your food processor.) Empty into a bowl and set aside for at least 1 hour.

Take 1 tablespoon of the mixture and shape it between your palms into a disk, about 2 inches in diameter. Repeat until all the mixture has been used.

Just before serving, heat ⅜-inch depth of oil in a large nonstick skillet, add a single layer of the falafels, and fry until golden and crisp on one side, then turn them over to crisp on the other side. Remove with a slotted spoon and drain on a plate lined with paper towels. Repeat until all the falafels have been fried. They are delicious served hot or at room temperature.

8 oz. dried, skinless fava beans, soaked overnight in cold water to cover

1 large onion, about 14 oz., coarsely chopped

2 garlic cloves, crushed

1 tablespoon ground cumin

1 tablespoon ground coriander

1 teaspoon ground allspice

¼ teaspoon cayenne pepper

¼ teaspoon baking powder

2½ cups fresh parsley, coarsely chopped

a handful of cilantro, coarsely chopped

groundnut or safflower oil, for deep-frying

MAKES ABOUT 20

RED BELL PEPPER ROULADE

2 large red bell peppers

6 oz. mozzarella cheese

8 large fresh basil leaves

1 tablespoon Pesto alla Genovese (page 181)

extra virgin olive oil

sea salt and freshly ground black pepper

EGGPLANT, SALAMI, AND ARTICHOKE

1 medium eggplant, about 8 oz.

6 tablespoons olive oil, plus extra for brushing

8 thin slices salami

4 artichokes marinated in oil, drained and halved

2 tablespoons freshly squeezed lemon juice

1 tablespoon capers, rinsed, drained, and chopped

sea salt and freshly ground black pepper

LEMON-MARINATED ZUCCHINI

3 medium zucchini

¼ cup olive oil, plus extra for brushing

2 tablespoons freshly squeezed lemon juice

1 tablespoon freshly grated Parmesan cheese

2 anchovies, rinsed and finely chopped

toothpicks

a ridged stovetop grill pan

SERVES 4

Antipasti literally means "before the meal" and are the delicious little appetizers that traditionally begin an Italian meal. The best antipasti are an appealing mix of colors, flavors, and textures, to whet the palate before the meal to come.

three marinated antipasti

To make the red bell pepper roulades, grill or broil the bell peppers until soft and black. Rinse off the charred skin, cut the peppers in quarters lengthwise, cut off the stalks, and scrape out the seeds. Cut the mozzarella into 8 thin slices. Put a slice inside each pepper strip, put a basil leaf on top and season well with salt and pepper. Roll up from one end and secure with a toothpick. Put the Pesto alla Genovese in a bowl and beat in enough olive oil to thin it to pouring consistency. Add the rolls and toss to coat. Cover and let marinate for at least 2 hours.

To make the eggplant antipasto, heat a ridged stovetop grill pan until hot. Cut the eggplant into 8 thin slices, brush lightly with olive oil, and cook for 2–3 minutes on each side. Put a slice of salami on each one, then a halved artichoke at one side. Fold the eggplant in half to cover the artichoke, secure with a toothpick and put in a shallow dish. Put the 6 tablespoons olive oil in a bowl, beat in the lemon juice, capers, salt, and pepper, then spoon over the eggplants. Cover and let marinate as above.

To make the lemon-marinated zucchini, cut the zucchini into long, thin slices, brush with olive oil, and cook on the same grill pan for 2–3 minutes on each side. Transfer to a shallow dish. Beat the olive oil, lemon juice, Parmesan, and anchovies together in a bowl, then pour over the zucchini. Cover and let marinate as above. Serve all three as mixed antipasti.

slow-roasted tomatoes on bruschetta with salted ricotta

8 large, ripe plum or round tomatoes

2 garlic cloves, finely chopped

1 tablespoon dried oregano

¼ cup extra virgin olive oil

2 oz. salted ricotta or feta cheese, thinly sliced

sea salt and freshly ground black pepper

basil leaves, to serve (optional)

BRUSCHETTA

4 thick slices country bread, preferably sourdough

2 garlic cloves, halved

extra virgin olive oil, for drizzling

SERVES 4

These firm but juicy roasted tomatoes burst with the flavor of the sun. They take no time to prepare but a long time concentrating their flavors in the oven—they smell fantastic while cooking! Plum tomatoes have less moisture in them and work well. You can use other vine-ripened varieties—just make sure they have some taste!

If using plum tomatoes, cut them in half lengthwise; if using round ones, cut them in half crosswise. Put them cut side up on a baking sheet. Mix the garlic and oregano with the olive oil, and season with salt and pepper. Spoon or brush this mixture over the cut tomatoes. Bake in a preheated oven at 325°F for about 2 hours, checking them occasionally. They should be slightly shrunk and still a brilliant red color. If they are too dark they will be bitter. Let cool.

To make the bruschetta, broil, toast, or pan-grill the bread on both sides until lightly toasted. Cut the bruschetta slices to size so that 2 tomato halves will sit on top of each one. Rub the top side of each slice with the cut garlic, then drizzle with olive oil.

Put 2 tomato halves on each bruschetta, sprinkle with the slivered cheese, and top with a basil leaf, if liked. Serve at room temperature.

1 Italian sfilatino or thin
French baguette, sliced into
thin rounds

extra virgin olive oil, for brushing

TAPENADE

6 oz. Greek-style black olives,
such as Kalamata, pitted

2 garlic cloves

3 canned anchovies, drained

2 teaspoons capers, drained

1 tablespoon extra virgin olive
oil, plus extra to cover

WHITE BEAN PURÉE

2 tablespoons olive oil

2 garlic cloves, finely chopped

1 teaspoon very finely chopped
fresh rosemary

1 small red chili, seeded
and finely chopped

1 lb. canned cannellini
beans, rinsed and drained

sea salt and freshly ground
black pepper

TO SERVE

chopped fresh parsley

SERVES 6–8

The combination of bland, creamy beans and sharp, rich, salty tapenade makes a sublime mouthful, especially when spread on crisp crostini. You can use any type of canned bean for this, but the whiter they are the prettier they look. If you like, chop up some more black olives and sprinkle them on the bean purée or crumble some crisply cooked bacon over the top for extra crunch.

white bean and black olive crostini

To make the tapenade, put the olives, garlic, anchovies, capers, and olive oil into a food processor and blend until smooth. Scrape out into a jar, cover with a layer of olive oil, and set aside.

Brush both sides of each slice of bread with olive oil and spread out on a baking sheet. Bake in a preheated oven at 375°F about 10 minutes until crisp and golden.

Meanwhile, make the white bean purée. Heat the oil in a small skillet and add the garlic. Cook gently for 2 minutes until golden but not brown. Stir in the rosemary and chili. Remove from the heat, add the beans and 3 tablespoons water. Mash the beans roughly with a fork and return to the heat until warmed through. Taste and season with salt and pepper.

Spread a layer of tapenade on the crostini followed by a spoonful of bean purée. Scatter with parsley and serve immediately.

caponata

Caponata is similar to ratatouille, but much more exotic. There are dozens of variations of this delectable dish from Sicily, which is usually served as an appetizer at room temperature. It improves with age, so make a big batch and keep in the refrigerator.

Sprinkle the eggplant with the salt, toss well, and let stand for 10 minutes. Drain and pat dry with paper towels.

Put the olive oil into a large, heavy-based saucepan and heat until very hot. Add the onion, garlic, olives, and capers. Stir over high heat for 2–3 minutes, then add the eggplant and continue to cook, stirring, over medium heat for another 8 minutes. Using a slotted spoon, transfer the mixture to a plate and set aside.

Add the oregano, marjoram, or thyme to the pan, then add the tomatoes, zucchini, tomato paste, sugar, and stock or water. Stir gently and bring to a boil. Reduce the heat and simmer for 8 minutes. Return the eggplant mixture to the pan and simmer gently until the flavors have mingled. The vegetables should still be intact, not mushy.

Dip the pan into a bowl of cold water to cool.

To serve, transfer to a bowl, sprinkle with parsley, and top with the extra sprigs of oregano, marjoram, or thyme, if using. Caponata may be served warm, cool, or cold, but not chilled.

1 eggplant, about 10 oz., cut into ½-inch cubes

1 tablespoon salt

¼ cup extra virgin olive oil

2 red onions, cut into 8 wedges each

4 garlic cloves, chopped

1 cup dry-cured green olives

¾ cup dry-cured black olives

⅓ cup capers in salt

2 teaspoons freshly chopped oregano, marjoram, or thyme leaves, plus extra sprigs, to serve (optional)

3 tomatoes, about 10 oz., cut into 8 wedges each

2 baby zucchini, about 8 oz., sliced crosswise

2 tablespoons tomato paste

2 teaspoons sugar

⅔ cup chicken or vegetable stock or water

4 tablespoons chopped fresh flatleaf parsley

SERVES 6–8

There are many versions of this recipe, but when served as a meze dish, the stuffing is usually a simple, aromatic mixture of rice, onions, and herbs. They are time consuming to make, but invite your friends around and enlist some help; the results are well worth the effort. Serve with other meze dishes, such as Moroccan-style Marinated Black Olives (page 13), Falafels (page 20), and Spicy Meat Pastries (page 38).

stuffed vine leaves

Bring a large saucepan of water to a boil and blanch the fresh vine leaves for 1–2 minutes in batches of 5–6 at a time. Remove with a slotted spoon and drain in a colander. They should just be wilted. If using preserved leaves, remember they are very salty—rinse first, then soak in a bowl of hot water for 3–5 minutes. Remove, rinse again, and drain in a colander.

To make the stuffing, put half the lemon juice in a large bowl. Add the rice, onions, scallions, dill, mint, parsley, olive oil, salt and pepper and stir well.

Line the base of a wide saucepan with 4 or 5 vine leaves. Place a vine leaf, rough side up, on a chopping board (handle carefully as they are fragile). Put a heaping teaspoon of the stuffing near the stalk end, fold the 2 opposite sides over the stuffing, and roll up tightly like a fat cigar. Repeat with the remaining leaves.

Arrange the stuffed vine leaves in tight circles in the saucepan with the loose ends underneath. Pour the olive oil and the remaining lemon juice over the top and set a small inverted plate on top to stop them opening up while cooking. Add the measured hot water, cover and simmer gently for 50 minutes.

Serve hot or at room temperature on a platter lined with fresh vine leaves, if available.

55 fresh vine leaves, plus extra to serve (optional), or 8 oz. preserved vine leaves

¼ cup extra virgin olive oil

2 cups hot water

STUFFING

freshly squeezed juice of 1 lemon, strained

1 cup long-grain white rice, rinsed

2 large onions, finely chopped (not grated)

5 scallions, including white parts, trimmed and thinly sliced

4 tablespoons fresh dill, finely chopped

2 tablespoons fresh mint, finely chopped

2 tablespoons finely chopped fresh flatleaf parsley

5 tablespoons extra virgin olive oil

sea salt and freshly ground black pepper

MAKES 50

48 small uncooked shrimp, about 20 oz., shelled and deveined, with tail shell left on

¼ cup extra virgin olive oil

8 garlic cloves, bruised

6 small dried chilies

8 small, fresh bay leaves

freshly squeezed juice of ½ lemon

sea salt

ALIOLI

5 garlic cloves, finely chopped

a large pinch of salt

½ cup extra virgin olive oil

2 teaspoons freshly squeezed lemon juice, plus extra to taste

½ cup safflower oil

fine sea salt and freshly ground white pepper

4 individual cazuelas (terra cotta ramekins), 4-5 inches in diameter, preheated in a hot oven

SERVES 4

This mouthwatering dish is a staple on many tapas menus in Spain. It is traditionally served sizzling hot in individual terra cotta bowls called cazuelas, accompanied by a small bowl of delicious alioli (garlic mayonnaise).

garlic shrimp

To make the alioli, pound the garlic and a large pinch of salt to a smooth, thick, creamy consistency with a mortar and pestle. Slowly drip in the olive oil, mixing with the pestle. Switch to a whisk and mix in the lemon juice, white pepper, and, little by little, half the safflower oil. Add 1-2 teaspoons cold water and whisk well while adding the remaining oil. The mixture will be very thick. Set aside for at least 30 minutes for the garlic to mellow, then add salt, pepper, and extra lemon juice to taste.

To prepare the shrimp, put them on a plate and sprinkle lightly with salt. Heat the olive oil in a skillet, add the garlic and fry until brown. Add the chilies, bay leaves, and shrimp all at once and fry without turning until the shrimp are crusted and curled on one side, then turn them over and crust the other side, about 3½ minutes in total.

Transfer to the preheated cazuelas, sprinkle with lemon juice, and top with a spoonful of alioli. Serve immediately while still bubbling hot.

clams with chili parsley sauce

2 lb. littleneck clams, scrubbed, rinsed, and drained

¼ cup extra virgin olive oil

1 teaspoon dried chili flakes

4 garlic cloves, chopped

1 onion, finely chopped

½ cup dry or sweet white vermouth

freshly ground black pepper

a handful of fresh parsley, chopped, plus 4–6 leaves, to serve (optional)

SERVES 4–6

Clam dishes in Italy are wonderful and this sweet shellfish is used in many different ways, all simple and delicious. Serve this as an appetizer with toasted ciabatta to mop up the sauce. Another classic dish is Pasta con le Vongole (page 187)—pasta with clam sauce.

Put the clams, olive oil, chili flakes, garlic, onion, vermouth, and black pepper into a large saucepan. Bring to a boil, cover tightly with a lid, reduce the heat, and let steam for about 4–6 minutes.

Stir in the chopped parsley and cover again. Turn off the heat, let steam for a further 1 minute, then serve, topped with a parsley leaf, if using.

Note Canned or bottled clams in the shell are widely available in Italian gourmet stores and are useful if you can't find any fresh clams. If using canned or bottled clams, drain the liquid into the pan, add all the remaining ingredients except the clams, bring to a boil, and reduce to about 1 cup. Add the drained clams, then steam just until the clams have been heated through. Serve as above.

8-oz. piece of sashimi-grade
tuna or swordfish or swordfish
loin (thin end)

1 cup arugula

freshly shaved Parmesan cheese

DRESSING

freshly squeezed juice of
3 lemons

⅔ cup extra virgin olive oil

1 garlic clove, finely chopped

1 tablespoon salted capers,
rinsed and chopped

a pinch of hot red pepper flakes

sea salt and freshly ground
black pepper

SERVES 4

This dish requires good-quality sashimi-grade tuna or swordfish, which a good fish seller should be able to provide. Chilling or lightly freezing it makes it firm enough to slice very thinly. As soon as the slices hit plates at room temperature, they become meltingly soft.

fresh tuna carpaccio

Trim the tuna of any membrane or gristle. Wrap tightly in plastic wrap and freeze for about 1 hour, until just frozen but not rock solid.

Meanwhile, to make the dressing, put the lemon juice, olive oil, garlic, capers, chili flakes, salt, and pepper in a bowl and whisk until emulsified.

Unwrap the tuna and slice it thinly with a sharp, thin-bladed knife. Arrange the slices so they completely cover 4 large plates. Spoon the dressing over the top. Add a tangle of arugula and sprinkle with Parmesan shavings, then serve.

1⅓ cups all-purpose flour

½ teaspoon sea salt

2 tablespoons extra virgin olive oil

1 egg yolk, lightly beaten

FILLING

3–4 tablespoons extra virgin olive oil

1 large onion, finely chopped

6½ oz. lean ground lamb

1 teaspoon ground allspice

1 teaspoon ground cumin

a large pinch of ground cinnamon

freshly squeezed juice of 1 lemon

3 tablespoons raisins, rinsed

⅔ cup hot water

3 tablespoons finely chopped fresh mint leaves

2 tablespoons pine nuts, toasted in a dry skillet

sea salt and freshly ground black pepper

a round 3-inch pastry cutter

MAKES ABOUT 30

Packed with sweet and sour flavors, these intricate little pastries are known as sambusak in Greece where they are often served as part of a mixed meze. Traditionally fried, they can also be baked.

spicy meat pastries

To make the pastry, sift the flour and salt into a bowl. Make a well in the center, add the olive oil, and mix with your fingers. Add 6 tablespoons water and knead until a neat ball is formed. Cover with plastic wrap and let rest for 30 minutes.

To make the filling, heat the olive oil in a saucepan, add the onion and sauté until it turns light brown, about 10 minutes. Increase the heat and add the lamb, turning and breaking up the lumps until all the moisture has evaporated and it starts to sizzle. Add the allspice, cumin, cinnamon, salt, and pepper and brown for 2–3 minutes. Add the lemon juice, raisins, and the hot water, then cover and cook for 20 minutes. It should be a fairly dry mixture by then. Add the mint and pine nuts and set aside.

Divide the pastry in half. Put one piece on a lightly-floured surface and roll out thinly to a circle about 12 inches in diameter, turning the pastry frequently. Cut out rounds with the pastry cutter. Gather the remaining pastry from around the discs and add it to the remaining portion of pastry. Knead until soft again, cover, and set aside.

Have a small bowl of cold water by you. Put 1 teaspoon of filling in the middle of a round of pastry. Dip a finger in the water and wet the edges, then fold half of the pastry over the other half making a half-moon shape. Press the edges firmly to seal and put it on an oiled baking sheet. Repeat until all the rounds have been used. Roll out the remaining pastry, cut out more rounds, and repeat the process.

Brush the tops with the egg yolk and bake in a preheated oven at 400°F for 10–12 minutes until light golden.

bresaola and arugula
with olive oil and parmesan

Bresaola is Italian cured, air-dried beef—flavorful, deep crimson, lean, and succulent. Preferably it should be cut from a piece, sliced very thinly, but it is also available pre-sliced, in packages. This combination of mellow, salty meat with the sharp, savory taste of Parmesan and best quality extra virgin olive oil is simple, but wonderful.

12–16 thin slices of bresaola

2 oz. Parmesan cheese, in a piece

a large handful of arugula

4–6 teaspoons extra virgin olive oil

SERVES 4

Arrange the slices of bresaola on 4 serving plates.

Using a vegetable peeler or sharp knife, shave off thin curls of the Parmesan and drop them on top of the bresaola.

Scatter the arugula over the top, then drizzle with the olive oil. Serve immediately.

Tapas bars, or tascas, are found all over Spain and serve an impressive range of little dishes to accompany a glass of sherry or wine. The word tapa *means lid and originally referred to a slice of bread placed on top of a glass to keep the flies away. These delectable fritters should be served very hot, with lots of napkins, toothpicks, and a bowl of coarse sea salt.*

potato fritters with chorizo

Boil the potatoes in a saucepan of salted water until soft, drain through a colander and cover with a cloth for about 5 minutes to let them dry out. Transfer to a bowl, mash in the flour, and season with a little black pepper. Mix in the egg yolks, then stir in the chorizo.

Put the egg whites in a separate bowl and whisk until soft peaks form. Fold into the mashed potatoes a little at a time.

Fill a saucepan or deep-fryer one-third full with oil, or to the manufacturer's recommended level. Heat to 350°F.

Working in batches of 6, take heaped teaspoons of the mixture and lower into the hot oil. Fry each batch for 3 minutes until evenly golden, turning them over halfway through (if they brown too quickly they will not have a good texture in the center). Keep the oil temperature constant. As each batch is done, drain on paper towels and keep them warm in a preheated oven 350°F until all have been cooked. Serve hot.

1 lb. potatoes, peeled and cut lengthwise into thick fingers

1 tablespoon self-rising flour

2 large eggs, separated, plus 1 egg white

4 oz. chorizo, skinned and chopped into small pieces

sea salt and freshly ground black pepper

olive or safflower oil, for deep-frying

MAKES ABOUT 24

Versions of this handsome, delicious dish are found all over Spain, the Basque country, and the South of France. Geographical origins will dictate the exact ingredients and treatment—but bell peppers, garlic, tomatoes, ham, and often eggs are essentials, as is fruity, robust olive oil. Try crumbling in some dried chilies for a spicier version.

piperrada

¼ cup extra virgin olive oil

1 Spanish onion, sliced into rings

3 garlic cloves, sliced

2 red bell peppers, halved, seeded, and sliced

2 yellow bell peppers, halved, seeded, and sliced

2 ripe red tomatoes, peeled and sliced

6 eggs

4 slices jamon Serrano ham or prosciutto

1 dried red chili, crumbled (optional)

sea salt and freshly ground black pepper

SERVES 6–8

Heat 3 tablespoons of the oil in a heavy skillet over a medium heat. Add the onions and garlic and sauté until soft and fragrant but not brown. Add the bell peppers and tomatoes. Cover the skillet, reduce the heat, and cook to form a soft thick purée, about 8–12 minutes. Season to taste.

Break the eggs into a bowl, add salt and pepper, and stir with a fork. Using a spatula, push a space clear near the center of the pan. Add the remaining oil to the space, then pour in the eggs. Stir gently over medium heat until semi-set. Turn off the heat.

Fold the slices of ham into rosettes or pleats, then add to the skillet. Crumble over some hot chili, if using, and serve straight from the skillet.

Note Rounds or triangles of bread fried in olive oil are often served as an accompaniment to piperrada.

grilled bell pepper frittata

1 small red bell pepper, quartered and seeded

1 small yellow bell pepper, quartered and seeded

1 small green bell pepper, quartered and seeded

2 tablespoons ricotta or mascarpone cheese

6 large eggs

2 tablespoons fresh thyme leaves

2 tablespoons extra virgin olive or safflower oil

1 large red onion, sliced

1 tablespoon balsamic vinegar

2 garlic cloves, crushed

sea salt and freshly ground black pepper

an 8-inch heavy skillet (measure the base, not the top)

SERVES 2–3

A frittata should be cooked slowly and be only lightly colored, and still slightly moist when served. The Italians usually flip them to finish cooking, but often a recipe will suggest quickly flashing the frittata under the broiler or putting it in a hot oven just to set the top. They can also be cut into squares and served cold, if desired.

Put the bell peppers skin side up under a preheated broiler and cook until the skins have blackened. Transfer to a bowl, cover, and let cool. This will steam off the skins, making them easier to remove.

Put the cheese in a large bowl, add 1 egg and mix to loosen the cheese. Whisk in the remaining eggs with a fork. Season with salt, pepper, and thyme and stir into the cheese mixture.

Peel the blackened skins off the peppers and rinse under cold running water. Pat dry with paper towels and cut into thick strips. Stir into the bowl.

Heat half the oil in the skillet, add the sliced onion and balsamic vinegar, and cook over gentle heat for about 10 minutes until softened. Add the garlic and cook for 1 minute.

Using a slotted spoon, add the onion to the egg mixture and stir. Add the remaining oil to the skillet and heat gently. Pour the frittata mixture into the pan and let cook over low heat until almost set, puffy, and light golden-brown on the underside.

Finish under a preheated broiler or put a plate or flat saucepan lid on top of the pan and invert the pan so the frittata drops onto the plate or lid. Slide back into the pan and cook for 30–60 seconds. Transfer to a serving plate and serve hot or at room temperature, cut into wedges.

soups and salads

There are numerous variations of this chilled, tomato-based soup from Spain. Originally, it was a peasant dish that made use of the three basic ingredients much revered in Spain—oil, water, and bread, and other ingredients were added according to what was available. If you chill it, put it in a container with a tight-fitting lid so the flavors don't mingle with anything else in the refrigerator.

gazpacho

Put ¼ of the chopped onion in a small bowl and add ¼ teaspoon of the sugar, ½ teaspoon of the vinegar, and 3 tablespoons cold water and set aside. Reserve ¼ of the prepared red and green bell peppers and put in small bowls. These small bowls will be served as garnishes at the end.

To make the other garnishes, put the unpeeled, chopped cucumber, croutons, and chopped tomatoes in separate small bowls and set aside.

To make the gazpacho, put the bread, garlic, and remaining sugar in a flat dish, sprinkle with the remaining vinegar and 1 cup cold water, and let soak.

Cut the peeled tomatoes in half and cut out the hard core. Put a strainer over a bowl and seed the tomatoes into the strainer. Push the seeds with a ladle to extract all the juices. Put the juices in a blender and discard the seeds. Add the soaked bread mixture and half the tomatoes. Blend until smooth and pour into a bowl.

Put the remaining tomatoes, the remaining onion, and ½ cup ice water in the blender. Pulse 8 times to get a medium chunky effect, then pour into the bowl. Put the remaining chopped bell peppers, coarsely chopped cucumber, olive oil, salt, and ⅔ cup ice water in the blender and pulse 8 times. Add to the bowl and stir in Tabasco, if using. Chill for up to 2 hours.

If you like ice added, serve with crushed ice cubes. Put the bowls of garnishes on the table for guests to sprinkle over the gazpacho.

1 large sweet Spanish onion, finely chopped

1½ teaspoons sugar

4 tablespoons white wine vinegar

1 large red bell pepper, peeled with a vegetable peeler and coarsely chopped

1 large green bell pepper, peeled with a vegetable peeler and coarsely chopped

3 slices country-style bread, with crusts, about 4 oz.

3 garlic cloves, crushed

5 lb. ripe tomatoes, peeled

5 inches cucumber, peeled and coarsely chopped

6 tablespoons extra virgin olive oil

fine sea salt

a splash of Tabasco (optional)

ice (optional)

GARNISHES

2 inches cucumber, unpeeled, finely chopped

½-inch bread croutons, sautéed in olive oil infused with garlic

2 ripe tomatoes, finely chopped

SERVES 6

1½ lb. asparagus

3 tablespoons extra virgin olive oil

1 tablespoon butter

2 leeks, well washed and thinly sliced

1 onion, finely chopped

1 quart chicken stock

freshly grated nutmeg

⅔ cup heavy cream

sea salt and freshly ground white pepper

a mouli (optional)

SERVES 4

Asparagus is regarded as a delicacy in many parts of France and Spain and is often simply steamed and served with a vinaigrette for dipping. This delicious, creamy soup is another wonderful way to cook and eat it.

cream of asparagus soup

Cut the tips off 8 asparagus spears and reserve. Chop the rest into ¾-inch pieces.

Heat the olive oil and butter in a saucepan, add the leeks and onion, cover, and sauté over gentle heat for 10 minutes. Add the chopped asparagus, stock, and a pinch of nutmeg, season well with salt and pepper, and simmer for 10 minutes.

Transfer to a blender, purée until smooth, then, using the back of a ladle, push through a strainer set over a bowl. Alternatively, use a mouli. Add two-thirds of the cream to the bowl and stir well. Return the soup to the saucepan and heat gently when ready to serve (do not let boil).

Cook the reserved asparagus tips in boiling water until just tender. Ladle the soup into bowls, spoon the remaining cream on top, add the asparagus tips and another pinch of nutmeg, then serve.

soupe au pistou

Pistou is the Provençal version of Italian pesto; and to make it you need a big bunch of fresh basil. This version of the soup is quicker to cook than the traditional one and can be made with your choice of Mediterranean vegetables.

To make the pistou, put the basil and garlic in a food processor and blend as finely as possible. Add enough olive oil in a steady stream to form a loose paste. Set aside.

Heat the measured olive oil in a small skillet, add the onion wedges, and fry gently on both sides until softened. Cook the potato and soup pasta in boiling salted water until tender. Drain. Blanch the carrots, Brussels sprouts, bell pepper, and peas in boiling salted water until tender but crisp, about 3–5 minutes. Drain and refresh in cold water.

Bring the stock to a boil and add salt and pepper, the pasta, vegetables, and cannellini beans. Simmer for 2 minutes or until heated through.

Serve in heated soup plates, with a separate bowl of pistou for guests to stir into their soup.

¼ cup extra virgin olive oil

1 red onion, cut into wedges

1 large potato, cut into ½-inch cubes

a handful of soup pasta, such as orecchiette (or the traditional vermicelli)

4 baby carrots, halved or quartered lengthwise

2 cups Brussels sprouts, halved, or baby zucchini, cut into thick slices

1 red bell pepper, halved, seeded, and sliced

1¾ cups shelled green peas

1 quart chicken or vegetable stock

1 cup cooked cannellini beans, rinsed and drained

sea salt and freshly ground black pepper

PISTOU

leaves from 1 large bunch of basil

2 garlic cloves, crushed

olive oil

SERVES 4

avgolemono

1 cup long-grain white rice

1½ quarts chicken or
vegetable stock

2 large eggs

grated peel and freshly
squeezed juice of
2 large lemons

sea salt and freshly ground
white pepper

TO SERVE

a large handful of fresh flatleaf
parsley, finely chopped

1 small lemon, thinly sliced
(optional)

SERVES 4

*The name of this classic Greek soup literally means "egg-lemon."
It is incredibly fresh and very easy to prepare. If you're serving it
to guests, prepare the stock and rice first, then complete the dish
just before serving.*

Wash the rice well to remove the starch, then drain in a strainer.

Put the stock in a large saucepan and bring to a boil. Add the rinsed rice and
return to a boil. Reduce to a simmer and cook for about 20 minutes or until the
rice is tender. Season with salt and pepper.

Put the eggs in a small bowl and whisk well. Stir in the lemon juice and
1 tablespoon water.

Remove the soup from the heat and whisk one ladle of soup into the egg
mixture. Add 2 more ladles, whisking again. Return the egg mixture to the
pan and stir well.

Serve the soup in wide, shallow bowls, with a sprinkling of parsley and
a little lemon peel. Float a few paper-thin slices of lemon on top if you like.

Note Do not reboil the soup after adding the eggs, or they will scramble.

This superb, ancient recipe from Provence excites huge passion and interest. Bouillabaisse consists of fragrant fish chunks poached in a saffron-enhanced broth. The dish is served as two courses: first the broth is spooned over toasted bread croûtes topped with rouille (rust) sauce, which enriches the soup; next the fish itself is eaten. It is undoubtedly a triumph, so do devote several hours to making it.

bouillabaisse

To make the aïoli, put the garlic, salt, egg, and egg yolks in a food processor and blend until creamy. Gradually pour in the olive oil until the mixture is thick and emulsified. Add the lemon juice and blend briefly to combine. Set aside.

Heat half the olive oil in a large, flameproof casserole dish, add the onions, leeks, garlic, and tomatoes and sauté until golden and wilted. Add the thyme, fennel, and orange peel. Add the boiling water and the remaining oil, then add the fish and shellfish (except the mussels or clams) and half the saffron.

Return to a boil, reduce the heat, and simmer for 10–12 minutes or until the fish is opaque. Add the mussels and clams, if using, and cook for 3–4 minutes until they open. Discard any that don't.

Pour the pan contents through a colander into a large bowl. Lift out the fish into a large, heated tureen or serving dish. Using a slotted spoon, press down on the onions, fennel, thyme, and tomatoes in the colander, then discard them.

Pour the broth back into the rinsed pan, bring to a boil, and cook over very high heat for 5 minutes until emulsified, then beat in half the aïoli. Add the hot potatoes and stir in the Pernod, if using. Pour one-quarter of the mixture over the fish.

Put a croûte on the side of each soup bowl, then add a generous spoonful of aïoli to each. Mix the remaining aïoli with the harissa and remaining saffron to create a scarlet rouille sauce. Add a spoonful of rouille to the croûtes. Ladle hot soup into each dish.

When the soup is finished, serve the fish and hot potatoes with any remaining aïoli and rouille.

¼ cup extra virgin olive oil

2 large onions, quartered

2 leeks, cut into 2-inch chunks

4 garlic cloves, chopped

2 large red tomatoes, peeled, quartered, and seeded

a bunch of fresh thyme, about 2 oz.

1 fennel bulb, quartered

8-inch strip of orange peel

2 quarts boiling water

2 lb. mixed fish fillets, such as halibut, grouper, red snapper, sea bass, and cod, cut into 1½-inch chunks

2 lb. mixed shellfish, such as small crabs, mussels, clams, and shrimp

a large pinch of saffron threads

1 lb. boiled new potatoes

1 tablespoon Pernod (optional)

¼ cup harissa paste or other hot chili paste

1 baguette, sliced and oven-toasted to make croûtes

AIOLI

6–8 large garlic cloves, crushed

½ teaspoon sea salt

1 egg, plus 2 egg yolks

1 cup extra virgin olive oil

1–2 tablespoons freshly squeezed lemon juice

SERVES 4–6

This classic salad comes from the Isle of Capri in the Bay of Naples, where it is known as Insalata Caprese. It combines three ingredients that work beautifully in harmony with each other: mozzarella (preferably soft, creamy mozzarella di bufala), red, ripe tomato, and plenty of fresh basil. To make this salad really sing of sunny Capri, use the best possible ingredients and be generous with them.

tomato, mozzarella, and basil salad

Cut the mozzarella and tomatoes into slices about ¼ inch thick. Arrange the tomato slices on a large plate and season with salt and pepper. Put 1 slice of mozzarella on each slice of tomato and top with a basil leaf. Tear up the remaining basil and scatter over the top. Drizzle with a generous amount of olive oil just before serving.

This salad must be made at the last moment to prevent the tomatoes from weeping and the mozzarella from drying out. Serve at room temperature, never chilled, as this would kill the flavors.

Variation Although not strictly Italian, sliced avocado is a delicious addition. Halve and peel one ripe avocado, remove the pit and slice the flesh, then intersperse the slices of avocado with the tomato and mozzarella.

2 balls of buffalo mozzarella, 5 oz. each

2 large, ripe tomatoes, roughly the same size as the balls of mozzarella

2 oz. fresh basil leaves

about ½ cup extra virgin olive oil

sea salt and freshly ground black pepper

SERVES 4

In Sicily, the land of orange and lemon groves, this salad is often served after grilled fish—especially in the region around Palermo. It is a perfect example of the Sicilian passion for sweet and savory combinations and is very refreshing.

orange, frisée, and black olive salad

To make the dressing, put the orange peel and juice, olive oil, basil, olives, and sun-dried tomatoes in a large bowl. Mix well, season with salt and pepper, and set aside to develop the flavors.

Peel the oranges with a sharp knife, removing all the skin and white pith. Cut out the segments. Set aside in a bowl. Finely slice the onion, using a very sharp, thin-bladed knife. Immediately toss the onion and oranges in the dressing to prevent discoloration. Let marinate in a cool place for 15 minutes.

Put the frisée on a plate and pile the dressed orange and onion mixture in the center, spooning over any remaining dressing. Serve immediately.

2 oranges

1 red onion

4 oz. frisée or escarole

DRESSING

finely grated peel and freshly squeezed juice of 1 orange

6 tablespoons extra virgin olive oil

2 tablespoons thinly sliced fresh basil

2 tablespoons finely chopped, pitted, Greek-style, oven-dried black olives

2 sun-dried tomatoes in oil, finely chopped

sea salt and freshly ground black pepper

SERVES 4

salad of belgian endive and blue cheese

8 oz. blue cheese, such as Spanish Cabrales or Picón, or French Roquefort

⅓ cup light cream

6 heads of Belgian endive or other crisp lettuce

3 tablespoons shelled walnuts, toasted in a dry skillet and roughly broken

¼ teaspoon hot Spanish paprika

SERVES 4

This delicious Spanish salad is a mouthwatering combination of blue cheese, Belgian endive, and walnuts. A dusting of pimentón adds an extra piquancy. Serve with chunks of crusty bread to mop up the creamy cheese dressing.

Put three-quarters of the blue cheese in a bowl, then add the cream little by little, mixing to a smooth sauce.

Trim the bases from the endive. Either cut them in half lengthwise or separate the leaves. Add to the bowl of dressing. Sprinkle with the walnuts and crumble the remaining cheese over the top. Dust with paprika and serve.

Note Spanish paprika (*pimentón*) is available in three forms; *pimentón dulce* is mild and sweet, *pimentón picante* is spicy hot, while *pimentón agridulce* is bittersweet. There are also smoked versions which are made from chilies hung whole in traditional mud houses above oak fires that burn for 10–15 days. All these varieties are available in gourmet stores.

Greek salads are so much part of the easy, Mediterranean style of eating—crisp lettuce, crumbly feta cheese, fragrant herbs, vinegary olives, and salty anchovies thrown together in a bowl. Use unpitted Kalamata olives, if possible, as they have more flavor than other kinds, but warn your guests in case they're not expecting them.

1 iceberg lettuce, quartered and torn apart

about 8 oz. feta cheese, crumbled into big pieces or cut into cubes

about 6 oz. Kalamata olives

2 red onions, thinly sliced

2 Kirby cucumbers, halved lengthwise, then thinly sliced diagonally

4 large tomatoes, cut into chunks

8 anchovy fillets, or to taste*

a few sprigs of oregano, torn

a few sprigs of mint, torn

DRESSING

⅓ cup extra virgin olive oil

2 tablespoons freshly squeezed lemon juice

sea salt and freshly ground black pepper

SERVES 4

greek salad

Put the lettuce in a large bowl. Add the cheese, olives, onions, cucumbers, and tomatoes.

To make the dressing, put the olive oil, lemon juice, salt, and pepper in a jug or bowl and beat with a fork, then pour over the salad. Alternatively sprinkle the dressing ingredients onto the salad separately.

Top the salad with the anchovies, oregano, and mint, and serve.

Note Look out for big cans of salted anchovies in Greek markets and gourmet stores—wheels of whole fish arranged nose to tail which you rinse and fillet yourself. If unavailable, use canned anchovy fillets.

warm mediterranean puy lentil salad

This is a salad for all seasons, which uses the quintessential Mediterranean flavorings of olive oil, lemon, garlic, and parsley. It works wonderfully served warm or cold and is bound to become a regular feature on your table.

Put the cherry tomatoes on a lightly oiled baking sheet and cook in a preheated oven at 250°F for 40 minutes.

Put the lentils in a saucepan. Add the lemon peel and juice, bay leaf, garlic, and enough water to cover. Stir, bring to a boil, then simmer for 40 minutes or until the lentils are soft.

Drain the lentils thoroughly and transfer to a large bowl. Add the tomatoes, onion, olives, parsley, olive oil, salt, and pepper. Toss gently, then serve topped with slices of Parmesan.

Note This is not only a great salad but, with various additions, can also be served as a whole meal in various ways. Try adding bacon or ham when cooking the lentils, or some spicy sausage just before you mix everything together.

10 cherry tomatoes

1½ cups Puy lentils or other brown lentils

grated peel and freshly squeezed juice of 1 lemon

1 fresh bay leaf

2 garlic cloves, chopped

2 red onions, diced

½ cup pitted green olives

a bunch of fresh flatleaf parsley, coarsely chopped

¼ cup extra virgin olive oil

sea salt and freshly ground black pepper

4 oz. Parmesan or mozzarella cheese, to serve

SERVES 4

grilled mixed vegetable salad with balsamic herb dressing

1 medium zucchini

1 medium eggplant

1 large red bell pepper, halved and seeded

⅔ cup extra virgin olive oil

2 small red onions, quartered

6 oz. cherry tomatoes

2 teaspoons balsamic vinegar

1 garlic clove, crushed

3 tablespoons chopped mixed fresh herbs, such as parsley, basil, marjoram, or oregano, plus extra to serve

sea salt and freshly ground black pepper

SERVES 4

This is one of the easiest ways to cook and serve a selection of Mediterranean vegetables for a large number of people. Broiling the vegetables concentrates their flavors, and a touch of aged balsamic vinegar cuts through their sweetness. Don't cut the vegetables too small—this salad should be robust and chunky.

Cut the zucchini, eggplant, and the bell pepper halves into large, bite-size pieces. Transfer to a large bowl, add 6 tablespoons olive oil and toss well. Season to taste with salt and pepper.

Line a broiler pan with aluminum foil and spoon in the vegetables. Add the onions and spread out the vegetables in an even layer (don't overcrowd the pan or they will stew). Broil under a preheated hot broiler for 4–5 minutes or until the edges of the vegetables start to catch. Stir well, add the tomatoes, and broil for a further 5 minutes until the vegetables are brown and cooked but not mushy.

Meanwhile, beat the remaining olive oil with the balsamic vinegar, garlic, and herbs. Pour the dressing over the vegetables, toss lightly, and transfer to a serving dish. Cover and set aside for at least 30 minutes to let the flavors infuse. Serve sprinkled with extra herbs. Do not serve chilled as this will ruin the flavor.

½ cup bulghur wheat

2 tomatoes, halved, cored, and chopped, with the juices reserved

1 red onion or shallot, finely chopped and soaked in a little lemon juice

½ cucumber, peeled, seeded, and cut into cubes

2 tablespoons extra virgin olive oil

a pinch of cayenne pepper

1 teaspoon ground sumac or the freshly squeezed juice of ½ lemon*

a bunch of fresh flatleaf parsley

a bunch of fresh mint

sea salt and freshly ground black pepper

lemon and lime wedges, to serve

SERVES 2–4

This Turkish salad of bulghur wheat and herbs is similar to the more familiar Lebanese tabbouleh. Chop the mint last and add it to the salad just before serving, to prevent it turning black. Traditionally, this salad is served with pickled vegetables on boiled vine leaves, but it also works well served simply with lemon and lime wedges.

mint and parsley salad

Put the bulghur in a bowl and cover with ⅔ cup cold water. Let stand for about 40 minutes to absorb the liquid.

Put the bulghur in a strainer and squeeze out any excess water. Transfer to a serving bowl, then add the tomatoes and their juices, onion, cucumber, olive oil, cayenne, salt, pepper, and half the sumac.

Remove the leaves from the parsley and mint and chop them coarsely. Add to the salad, toss gently, and sprinkle with the remaining sumac. Serve with lemon and lime wedges.

*Note The reddish-purple sumac berry is a spice tasting a little of lemons. It is sold finely ground and is available from Middle Eastern stores and specialty spice markets. If you can't find it, add the freshly squeezed juice of ½ lemon.

1–2 large garlic cloves, crushed

1 tablespoon sherry vinegar or
white wine vinegar

⅓ cup extra virgin olive oil

4 cups cooked cannellini beans,
rinsed and drained

2 red onions, thinly sliced, or
6 small scallions, sliced

14-oz. can good-quality tuna

a few handfuls of fresh basil

sea salt and freshly ground
black pepper

SERVES 6

This delicious antipasti of tuna and beans is a useful recipe when you're running low on fresh ingredients. Any dolphin-friendly canned tuna is fine, although top-quality French or Italian tuna, usually sold in jars, rather than cans, makes a special treat. Cannellini beans can be delicate, so toss them gently.

tonno e fagioli

Put the garlic on a chopping board, crush with the flat of a knife, add a large pinch of salt, then mash to a paste with the tip of the knife. Transfer to a bowl, add the vinegar and 2 tablespoons of the olive oil, and beat with a fork.

Add the beans and onion and toss gently. Taste, then add extra olive oil and vinegar to taste.

Drain the tuna and separate into large chunks. Add to the bowl and turn gently to coat with the dressing. Top with the basil and some black pepper.

salade niçoise

The famous Salade Niçoise was originally composed of crudités with eggs and anchovies. Now served in cafés, restaurants, and snack bars from New Zealand to Newfoundland, it is often made badly, with key ingredients left out or inappropriate ones added. Tuna, too costly for inclusion until recent times, can be fresh or canned, as long as it's of high quality. The anchovies can be salted, canned, or marinated, though marinated is really a Spanish innovation. Although this is a splendid entrée, it is also appealing as a side salad if served in small quantities.

1 head romaine lettuce,
3 romaine lettuce hearts,
or one iceberg lettuce, leaves
separated and halved if large

2 scallions or shallots, sliced

8–12 oz. good-quality canned
tuna, drained

2 oz. canned anchovies, or
24 marinated anchovy fillets,
halved lengthwise

12 black olives, such as Niçoise

4 hard-cooked large eggs,
peeled and quartered

a handful of small sprigs of
fresh flatleaf parsley or basil

4 ripe tomatoes, cut into
4–8 wedges

4 oz. green beans, halved,
or shelled fava beans,
freshly boiled

VINAIGRETTE

2 garlic cloves, crushed to a pulp

½ teaspoon sea salt

2 tablespoons wine vinegar

½ cup first cold-pressed extra
virgin olive oil

SERVES 4

Line a large salad bowl with the lettuce leaves. Add the scallions, tuna, anchovies, olives, egg quarters, parsley, tomatoes, and beans.

To make the vinaigrette, put the garlic, salt, vinegar, and olive oil in a bowl or bottle and beat or shake until emulsified. Pour over the salad just before serving.

The important thing with this chicken salad is to prepare it while the chicken is still warm. Pull the chicken breast into large pieces, rather than chopping it—it separates along the grain, tastes better, and is more tender.

warm chicken salad with harissa dressing

Put the tomatoes onto a baking sheet—if using vine tomatoes, put the whole vine on the sheet. Sprinkle with salt, olive oil, and the crushed garlic, then roast in a preheated oven at 400°F, until slightly blackened and starting to collapse. Let cool, but do not chill.

To make the harissa dressing, mix all of the ingredients in a salad bowl and beat with a fork.

While still warm, pull the chicken into long chunks. Add to the bowl, then add the greens, olives, and red onions and toss gently in the dressing.

Divide between 4 salad plates, add the tomatoes and serve.

Notes As unpitted olives have more flavor than pitted ones, pit and halve them yourself. Choose any kind—with garlic, chili, lemon, and herbs—whatever looks good on the day. Brands of harissa paste vary in heat, so add a little, taste, then add more if you prefer. Alternatively, use regular mustard.

2 baskets ripe cherry tomatoes, or 4 vine-ripened clusters of cherry or plum tomatoes

½ garlic clove, crushed

4 freshly-cooked chicken breasts

salad greens

20 large green or black olives, pitted and halved

2 red onions, halved, then cut into thin wedges lengthwise

sea salt

olive oil, for roasting

HARISSA DRESSING

⅓ cup extra virgin olive oil

1 tablespoon harissa paste

1 tablespoon cider or sherry vinegar

SERVES 4

This is one of the classics of French cooking and a perfect example of what is known as salade tiède or warm salad. It includes bitter leaves such as spinach, frisée, and escarole, and the salad is topped with crisp bacon, in this case the French lardons. The cooking juices from the pine nuts, garlic, and bacon are used to dress the salad.

french duck salade tiède

4 duck breasts

1 lb. baby spinach leaves

1 cup pine nuts

3 garlic cloves, thinly sliced

8 oz. bacon lardons, pancetta cubes, or thinly sliced smoked pancetta, as fatty as possible

olive oil, for frying

sea salt and freshly ground black pepper

VINAIGRETTE

6 tablespoons extra virgin olive oil

1 tablespoon red wine vinegar

sea salt and freshly ground black pepper

SERVES 4

Put the duck breasts skin side down in a skillet lightly brushed with olive oil. Sprinkle the flesh side with a little sea salt. Cook gently over low heat for 20–30 minutes to render out the fat—you will have to pour it off from time to time into a heatproof bowl. Take it slowly—the skin will gradually become crisp and golden and the fat line will almost disappear.

Meanwhile, make the vinaigrette. Put all of the ingredients in a small bowl and beat with a fork.

Turn the duck over and cook at high heat just to brown the flesh side—the interior should remain rare. Remove from the skillet and let rest for about 5 minutes if serving hot, or 20 minutes if serving cool. Carve crosswise on a wooden board, making sure each slice has its share of crackling.

Put the spinach in a bowl, add the vinaigrette, and toss lightly. Divide the leaves between 4 dinner plates or 8 appetizer plates.

Meanwhile, rinse and dry the skillet. Reheat, add about 2 tablespoons olive oil, then the pine nuts. Toast over low heat, tossing gently, until golden on all sides, about 1 minute. Take care—they burn easily. Remove from the skillet and let cool on a plate. Add the garlic to the pan and fry gently until crisp and golden brown. Remove to the same plate.

Add the bacon lardons and fry gently until crispy. Add the lardons to the salads, top with the pine nuts and garlic, then spoon the hot scented oil from the pan over the salads. Add freshly ground black pepper and serve.

fish and seafood

6 lb. fresh mussels

¼ cup extra virgin olive oil

3 garlic cloves, very finely chopped

3 onions, very finely chopped

¾ cup dry white wine

a good pinch of hot red pepper flakes

¼ cup chopped fresh flatleaf parsley

TO SERVE

lemon wedges

warm French bread

a cheesecloth-lined strainer

SERVES 6

In this classic French seafood dish, fresh mussels are cooked in white wine and flavored with garlic and chili. Take the pot to the table and ladle out the mussels first, then serve the delicious soupy juices to be mopped up with crusty bread. It is a is a dish to be shared with friends and savored.

moules marinière

Scrub the mussels well, knock off any barnacles, and pull off the beards. Discard any broken mussels and any that won't close when they are tapped on the work surface. Drain in a colander.

Heat the olive oil in a large saucepan. Add the garlic and onions and fry for 10 minutes until softened but not colored. Add the wine, red pepper flakes, and ¾ cup water, bring to a boil, and simmer for another 10 minutes. Add the mussels, cover, and cook over high heat for about 5 minutes, shaking the pan every now and then, until the mussels have opened. Discard any that remain closed. Strain the mussels through the cheesecloth-lined strainer set over a bowl or saucepan.

Keep the mussels warm in the strainer and boil the mussel liquid to reduce slightly. Stir in the parsley. Pile the mussels into warmed bowls, and pour over the hot broth. Serve with lemon wedges and bread to mop up the broth.

4 large garlic cloves, crushed

a bunch of fresh thyme
or rosemary

12 clams or other bivalves

12 mussels

about 4 tablespoons extra virgin
olive oil

2 large onions, cut into wedges
through the root

8 ripe, very red tomatoes,
peeled, halved, and seeded

2 lb. thick boneless white fish
fillets, such as cod

4–8 small whole fish, cleaned
and scaled (optional)

8 uncooked shrimp

4 cups boiling fish stock

sea salt and freshly ground
black pepper

crusty Italian bread, to serve

a cheesecloth-lined strainer

SERVES 4

A great dish with assertive flavors which is suitable for any occasion. You can alter the composition of this soup-stew according to what's available in your local market, but be sure to include thick white fish, shellfish, and shrimp. Serve with fresh Italian bread and a pitcher of light red wine.

neapolitan seafood stew

Put 1 cup water into a large saucepan and add 1 crushed garlic clove and half the herbs. Bring to a boil, then simmer for 2–3 minutes to extract the flavors. Add the clams, cover with a lid, and cook over high heat, shaking the pan from time to time. As they open, remove and put onto a plate, so they don't overcook. Discard any that don't open.

Add the mussels to the pan, cover with a lid, and cook until they open. Remove as they do so and add to the plate with the clams. Discard any that don't open. Strain the cooking stock through the cheesecloth-lined strainer into a bowl to remove the grit. Set aside.

Heat the olive oil in a large skillet, add the onion wedges, and cook until lightly browned on both sides. Reduce the heat and cook until softened. Stir in the remaining garlic and cook for a few minutes until golden. Add lots of black pepper, then add the tomatoes, the remaining herbs, both kinds of fish, and the shrimp. Pour in the stock and bring to boiling point. Reduce the heat and simmer for a few minutes until the fish turns opaque. Add the mussels, clams, and the strained mussel poaching liquid. Reheat, then add salt and pepper.

Ladle into 4 large, warmed bowls and serve with crusty Italian bread.

Paella is the perfect dish for outdoor parties—everything can be prepared ahead of time, then you just add the ingredients in a steady stream until the whole thing comes together. The smell is wonderfully enticing, so make enough for seconds. This is messy food, so have plenty of paper napkins around.

paella

3 tablespoons extra virgin olive oil

6 chicken thighs

6 oz. chorizo sausage, cut into chunks

2 garlic cloves, finely chopped

1 large onion, finely chopped

1 large red bell pepper, thinly sliced

2½ cups Spanish paella rice

¾ cup dry white wine

a good pinch of dried hot red pepper flakes

2 teaspoons sweet Spanish paprika (see page 65)

about 5 cups chicken stock

a large pinch of saffron strands, soaked in 3 tablespoons hot water

6 ripe tomatoes, quartered

12 whole uncooked shrimp, in their shells

1 lb. fresh mussels, scrubbed, rinsed, and debearded

1 cup fresh or frozen peas

¼ cup chopped fresh flatleaf parsley

sea salt and freshly ground black pepper

lime or lemon wedges, to serve

SERVES 6

Heat the olive oil in a paella pan or large, deep skillet. Add the chicken thighs and chorizo and brown all over, turning frequently. Stir in the garlic, onion, and red bell pepper and cook for about 5 minutes until softened.

Stir in the rice until all the grains are coated and glossy. Add the wine and let it bubble and reduce until almost disappeared. Stir in the red pepper flakes, paprika, chicken stock, and soaked saffron. Stir well, bring to a boil, and simmer gently for 10 minutes.

Stir in the tomatoes and shrimp and cook gently for 5 minutes before finally tucking the mussels into the rice and adding the peas. Cook for another 5 minutes until the mussels open (take out any that do not open after this time). At this stage, almost all the liquid will have been absorbed and the rice will be tender.

Sprinkle the parsley over the top and serve immediately, straight from the pan with a big pile of lime or lemon wedges on the side.

seafood with couscous

Couscous is probably Berber in origin and is found not only in North Africa, but also in Nice and other areas around the Mediterranean, such as Sicily, the home of this delicious recipe. The fish stew is ladled over aromatic cuscusu and the juices add their flavor to its fragrant charms. Modern "instant" or pre-cooked couscous is quick and easy because it needs only moistening and heating, unlike cooking traditional North African couscous which requires skill and is very time-consuming.

3 lb. assorted non-oily fish and shellfish, such as haddock, halibut, eel, crayfish, lobster, shrimp, crabs, mussels, and clams

1 teaspoon sea salt

4 garlic cloves, sliced

4 celery ribs, sliced

1 head of fennel, quartered

20 black peppercorns, crushed

12-inch strip of orange peel

12-inch strip of lemon peel

a bunch of oregano or thyme

1–2 tablespoons tomato paste

CUSCUSU

2½ cups coarse instant couscous

1 onion, sliced

2 green chilies, thinly sliced

2 tablespoons extra virgin olive oil

3 cups boiling seafood stock or hot water

1 teaspoon orange flower water (optional)

freshly squeezed juice of 1 orange

sea salt and freshly ground black pepper

SERVES 4–6

Cut the fish and shellfish into 1-inch chunks or, if small, leave whole. Put them in a very large flameproof casserole dish, add the salt, garlic, celery, fennel, peppercorns, and 2 cups water and bring to a boil. Stir in the orange and lemon peel, oregano, and enough tomato paste to make the liquid rosy. Reduce the heat to a simmer. Cover and cook for 10 minutes.

To prepare the cuscusu, put the couscous, onion, chilies, olive oil, salt, and pepper in a heatproof bowl. Pour in the boiling stock. Stir and leave for 5 minutes to plump up. Stir in the orange flower water, if using. When all the liquid has been absorbed, add the orange juice.

Put the cuscusu in deep bowls and serve the fish and its broth over the top.

1¼ lb. thick tuna steaks,
cut into 2-inch cubes

2–3 small red onions, quartered

2–3 mixed colored bell peppers,
seeded and sliced into
8 pieces each

5–6 sprigs of parsley, to serve

MARINADE

3 tablespoons olive oil

freshly squeezed juice of
1 large lemon

2 garlic cloves, crushed

1 green chili, seeded
and finely chopped

1 tablespoon dried oregano

1 teaspoon dried thyme

a handful of fresh parsley,
finely chopped

sea salt and freshly
ground black pepper

6 metal skewers

MAKES 6

Grilled fish is an integral part of Greek summer life and there is nothing more exhilarating than the aroma of barbecuing fish in the open air. Whenever the fishing boats bring in a large, glistening specimen, such as tuna or swordfish, it is inevitably made into kabobs by the local restaurants that evening. These tuna kabobs are a real treat at a barbecue and could be served with a selection of salads and dips, such as Greek Salad (page 66) and Babaghannouj (page 17).

grilled tuna kabobs

To make the marinade, put the olive oil, lemon juice, garlic, chili, oregano, thyme, parsley, salt, and pepper in a large bowl and beat well. Add the tuna pieces and stir to coat. Cover with plastic wrap and chill in the refrigerator for 2–3 hours, stirring occasionally.

Separate the onion quarters into 2–3 pieces each, according to their size. Remove the tuna cubes from the marinade. Starting with a piece of bell pepper, thread pieces of tuna, onion, and pepper onto a skewer, finishing with a piece of pepper. Repeat with the remaining skewers.

Grill over hot coals for 5–7 minutes on each side according to the strength of the fire, basting with the leftover marinade as they cook. Alternatively, cook under a preheated broiler on all sides, about 4 inches from the heat, for 6–8 minutes in total. Take care as tuna can become dry if overcooked.

Meanwhile, put the remaining marinade into a small saucepan and boil for 2–3 minutes. To serve, arrange the skewers on a platter with sprigs of parsley and drizzle some of the leftover marinade juices over the top.

spanish fishcakes

Bacalao (salt cod) is the classic base for these fishcakes. You can also use smoked cod, smoked haddock, or even smoked salmon instead, but if you use the traditional salt cod, it must be softened and desalted—put it in a bowl, cover with cold water, and keep in the refrigerator for 24 hours, changing the water every 4 hours.

Cook the potatoes in boiling salted water for 20 minutes. Drain well, return to the still-hot, empty saucepan and let dry.

Put the milk into a skillet, bring to a boil, add the fish, and poach gently until flaking and hot, about 6–8 minutes. Drain well, reserving the hot milk. Cool the fish, then skin, bone, and flake it.

Add the flaked fish to the saucepan, then the olive oil, egg, scallions, cilantro, salt, and pepper. Mix and mash to a dense texture, adding ½–1 tablespoon of the hot milk if necessary. Divide the mixture into 8–12 balls. Pat out into flat cakes, then coat in the seasoned flour.

Put 6 tablespoons olive oil in a nonstick skillet and heat to 375°F or until a ½-inch cube of bread browns in 35–45 seconds. Cook 3–4 fishcakes at a time for about 4 minutes on each side. Using a spatula and a slotted spoon, turn them carefully to avoid splashes. Drain on crumpled paper towels and keep hot while all the rest are cooked, adding some extra oil to the pan. Serve hot with lemon wedges.

1 lb. potatoes, halved lengthwise

1½ cups whole milk

12 oz. smoked haddock or cod, or desalted salt cod

2 tablespoons extra virgin olive oil

1 egg, beaten

4 scallions, chopped

1 small bunch of fresh cilantro, chopped, about ¼ cup

½ cup all-purpose flour seasoned with salt and pepper, to coat

olive oil, for frying

sea salt and freshly ground black pepper

lemon wedges, to serve

SERVES 4

12 fresh, fat sardines

olive oil, for brushing

lemon wedges, to serve

SALMORIGLIO SAUCE

2 tablespoons red wine vinegar

1–2 teaspoons sugar

finely grated peel and freshly squeezed juice of ½ lemon

4 tablespoons extra virgin olive oil

1 garlic clove, finely chopped

1 tablespoon crumbled dried oregano

1 tablespoon salted capers, rinsed, and chopped

a grill rack

SERVES 4

The smell of silvery blue sardines on a grill is unmistakable—it is one of the most appetizing scents in outdoor cooking. Sardines grill very well because they are an oily fish and are self-basting. There are wheel-shaped grilling racks especially designed for sardines. Great shoals of sardines are to be found in Mediterranean waters in May and June, when they are caught and eaten grilled, fried, or stuffed.

grilled sardines with salmoriglio sauce

To make the salmoriglio sauce, put the vinegar and sugar in a bowl and stir to dissolve. Add the lemon peel and juice. Beat in the olive oil, then add the garlic, oregano and capers. Set aside to infuse.

Using the back of a knife, scale the sardines, starting from the tail and working towards the head. Slit open the belly and remove the insides, then rinse the fish, and pat dry. Clip off any fins you don't want to see. Brush the fish with olive oil and arrange on the grill rack.

Cook under a hot broiler or over hot coals for about 3 minutes each side until sizzling hot and blackening. Serve with the salmoriglio spooned over the top, with lots of lemon wedges alongside.

2 whole fish, about 1½ lb. each, such as snapper, sea bass, or sea bream, scaled, cleaned, and fins trimmed

a few bay leaves

a few sprigs of fresh lemon thyme

2 tablespoons extra virgin olive oil, plus extra for basting

2 juicy lemons, halved

sea salt and freshly ground black pepper

CHERMOULA

1 teaspoon ground cumin

1 teaspoon ground coriander

a pinch of saffron threads

2 garlic cloves, chopped

1 teaspoon grated lemon peel

1 teaspoon mild Spanish paprika, preferably oak-smoked (see page 65)

2 tablespoons chopped, fresh flatleaf parsley

3 tablespoons chopped cilantro

freshly squeezed juice of 1 lemon

¼ cup extra virgin olive oil

cayenne or chili powder, to taste

sea salt and freshly ground black pepper

SERVES 4

Chermoula is a Moroccan spice paste or marinade fragrant with cilantro, garlic, lemon, and spices. It is a useful flavoring to know, as it is wonderfully adaptable, working equally well with fish, lamb, or chicken. Grilling the lemon releases the juice and mellows its flavor, making it perfect for squeezing over the grilled fish.

grilled fish with chermoula and grilled lemons

To make the chermoula, put the cumin, ground coriander, and saffron in a small saucepan and heat gently for 1 minute to release the aromas. Transfer to a small food processor or spice mill, then add the garlic, lemon peel, paprika, parsley, and cilantro and finely chop. Add the lemon juice and olive oil and blend to make a paste. Add a little cayenne, and salt and pepper to taste, cover, and set aside for 30 minutes.

Season the cavities of the fish with salt. Cut 4 or 5 diagonal, shallow slashes on each side of the fish and work a little chermoula into each cut. Lay the fish in a heatproof dish and stuff a few bay leaves and a little thyme into the cavities. Cover and let stand in the refrigerator for 30–60 minutes.

Season the fish with salt and pepper and sprinkle with the olive oil, then put under a preheated broiler, with the rack set about 4 inches from the heat. Grill for about 5 minutes on each side or until the fish is just cooked at the center—test with the tip of a pointed knife. When you turn the fish, add the lemon halves, cut side up, and baste them with a little extra oil. Grill until the cut surface of the lemons is nicely brown and the fish cooked. Serve the fish and lemons immediately with any remaining chermoula.

Note You can barbecue both fish and lemons. Use a special wire fish grill rack, which makes turning the fish easier. Oil the rack slightly and allow up to 10 minutes each side, depending on the heat of the coals and the size of the fish. Place the lemon halves directly on the barbecue or, alternatively, cook them on a ridged stove-top grill pan for 2–3 minutes until the cut surfaces are seared.

4 tuna steaks, 6 oz. each

1½ oz. Cheddar cheese, cut into 4 thin slices

sea salt and freshly ground black pepper

salad greens or buttered spinach, to serve

PAPRIKA CRUMBS

1 tablespoon olive oil

1 cup fresh white bread crumbs

1 tablespoon chopped fresh basil

½ teaspoon hot oak-smoked Spanish paprika (see page 65)

1 teaspoon tomato paste

½ teaspoon sugar

ROMESCO SAUCE

2 red bell peppers

½ cup olive oil

2 garlic cloves

1 red chili, seeded and sliced

7 oz. canned plum tomatoes

1½ tablespoons red wine vinegar

1 tablespoon ground hazelnuts

1 tablespoon ground almonds

1 teaspoon sea salt

SERVES 4

Tuna is a dark-fleshed fish that needs extra flavoring and takes well to hot paprika seasoning. The topping gives a moist and crunchy texture to a fish that can become dry and overcooked only too easily. Serve on a bed of salad greens or buttered spinach with romesco sauce— a hot, pungent, Catalan sauce thickened with ground almonds and hazelnuts, which is often served with fish and can also be used as a dip for crudités.

tuna with paprika crumbs and romesco sauce

To make the romesco sauce, blacken the peppers under a hot broiler, then put them in a paper bag, seal, and let steam for 10 minutes. Remove the skin, seeds, and membranes. Heat 1 teaspoon of the olive oil in a nonstick pan, lightly brown the garlic, then add the chili and tomatoes. Dry out the mixture over high heat so it starts to fry and even brown a little. Transfer to a blender, add the vinegar and remaining oil, and purée until smooth. Stir in the nuts to thicken the sauce and add salt to taste.

To make the paprika topping, put the olive oil in a skillet, add the bread crumbs, basil, paprika, tomato paste, sugar, and ½ teaspoon salt. Stir well and fry until crunchy. Remove from the skillet and let cool.

Season the tuna with salt and pepper, put on an oiled baking sheet and roast in a preheated oven at 475°F for 5 minutes.

Remove from the oven and turn over the steaks. Pile the paprika bread crumbs on top, then add the slice of cheese. Return to the oven and cook for a further 5 minutes or until the cheese has melted. Serve on a bed of salad greens or buttered spinach, with the sauce served separately.

braised sea bass with fennel and green olives

This is the perfect way to cook a whole firm-fleshed fish. It keeps the flesh moist, while the skin protects it. Fennel and olives are distinctive Mediterranean flavors and a winning combination.

Wash the fish inside and out and fill the cavity with sprigs of rosemary.

Cut the fennel bulbs in half lengthwise, cut out the cores, then slice thickly. Blanch in a large saucepan of salted boiling water for 5 minutes, then drain.

Put the olive oil, lemon juice, and herbs in a medium bowl and season with salt and pepper. Beat well, then stir in the fennel to coat. Tip this mixture into a shallow ovenproof dish. Put the fish on top of the fennel and pour over any remaining liquid. Tuck in the olives and pour the wine over the top.

Bake in a preheated oven at 425°F for 30 minutes. Baste with the juices and stir the fennel around, then turn off the oven and leave for about 5 minutes for the fish to "set." Serve immediately.

2½ lb. kg sea bass, grouper, or rock fish, scaled and cleaned

a few sprigs of rosemary

2 large fennel bulbs

⅔ cup extra virgin olive oil

freshly squeezed juice of 1 lemon

1 tablespoon dried oregano

3 tablespoons chopped fresh flatleaf parsley

8 large green olives, pitted

⅔ cup dry white wine

sea salt and freshly ground black pepper

SERVES 4

2 lb. monkfish tail

sea salt and freshly ground
black pepper

olive oil, for brushing

NIÇOISE SAUCE

1 cup canned tomatoes or
6 fresh tomatoes, peeled
and seeded

2 garlic cloves, crushed

2 tablespoons olive oil

½ cup white wine

1 cup fish stock

leaves from 2–3 sprigs of
thyme, chopped

leaves from 2–3 small sprigs
of tarragon, chopped

2 fresh sage leaves

1 bay leaf

sea salt and freshly ground
black pepper

TO SERVE

12 black olives, chopped

fennel fronds

an instant-read thermometer

SERVES 4

This is usually made with a whole, large monkfish tail but cutlets or even four individual tails may be used instead. Adding cream to the Niçoise sauce makes an unusual variation, while black olives and fennel fronds add color to the dish. Serve with rice.

roast gigot of monkfish with niçoise sauce

To make the Niçoise sauce, put the tomatoes, garlic, and olive oil in a saucepan, bring to a boil, reduce the heat, and simmer until they cook to a pulp—crush them from time to time. Add the wine and keep simmering until it has been absorbed by the tomatoes. Add the stock, thyme, tarragon, sage, bay leaf, salt, and pepper.

Peel the skin off the monkfish and cut away the loose membrane. Shorten the tail with scissors but do not cut into the flesh or it will shrink back and expose the bone as it cooks. Brush the fish with the oil and season with salt and pepper.

Spoon half the sauce into a roasting tin, rest the fish on it, and roast in a preheated oven at 350°F for 10 minutes. Turn the fish over and continue to cook until an instant-read thermometer registers 136°F, about 10 minutes. Transfer the fish to a serving dish and keep it warm.

Pour the roasting juices back into the saucepan of Niçoise sauce, bring to a boil, and simmer until reduced to a pulp. Add salt and pepper to taste.

Pour the sauce around the fish, add the olives and fennel fronds, and serve.

The rose and gold skin of the red snapper looks beautiful with the deep red of the blood oranges. If you can't find blood oranges, use regular oranges instead. Citrus fruits are often cooked with fish in Italy—their gentle acidity brings out the sweetness of the flesh. You could also add a tablespoon of wine to each serving if tempted. The aroma when you open the packages is wonderful.

red snapper and orange packages

4 small red snapper, 8 oz. each, carefully scaled, cleaned, and filleted

2 tablespoons extra virgin olive oil, plus extra for brushing

2 oranges, preferably blood oranges

8 fresh bay leaves

20 small black olives

sea salt and freshly ground black pepper

SERVES 4

Cut 4 rectangles of aluminum foil or parchment paper large enough to wrap each fish loosely. Brush with a little oil.

Grate the peel from the oranges into a bowl, then mix in the olive oil, salt, and pepper, and set aside. Peel the oranges as you would an apple, removing all the white pith, then slice the flesh thinly. Put 1 bay leaf in the cavity of each fish and 1 on top. Put a pile of orange slices on one side of each square of foil, using half the orange slices in total. Put the fish on the oranges and cover them with the remaining orange slices. Sprinkle with the oil and orange peel mixture, then add the olives. Season well with salt and pepper.

If you have a water sprayer, spritz the inside of the foil lightly. Fold the foil loosely over the fish and twist the edges together. Lift onto a baking sheet. Bake in a preheated oven at 375°F for 20 minutes.

Serve on warm plates, letting guests open their own packages.

hake in garlic sauce with clams

This fish dish is traditionally cooked in a cazuela—a wide, flat, terra cotta casserole dish, glazed except for the base. It has amazing heat-retaining properties and is excellent for dishes that rely on slow, even heat. If cooking on top of the stove, use a heat-diffusing mat.

Put the clams and wine in a saucepan over high heat. As they open, remove them to a bowl and cover with plastic wrap. Discard any that don't open. Pour the cooking juices through the cheesecloth-lined strainer and set aside. Put the fish on a plate, sprinkle with salt, and leave to rest for 10 minutes.

Put the oil and garlic in a heavy skillet and heat gently so the garlic turns golden slowly and doesn't burn. Remove the garlic with a slotted spoon and keep until ready to serve.

Pour about two-thirds of the oil into a jug and add the fish to the oil left in the pan. Cook over very low heat, moving the pan in a circular motion—keep taking it off the heat so it doesn't cook too quickly (the idea is to encourage the oozing of the juices instead of letting them fry and burn). Add the remaining oil little by little as you move the pan, so an emulsion starts to form. When all the oil has been added, remove the fish to a plate and keep it warm. Put the pan back on the heat, add the reserved clam juices and stir to form a creamy sauce.

Return the fish to the pan, add the chopped parsley, and continue to cook until the fish is tender, about 5 minutes. Just before serving, add the clams and heat through. Serve sprinkled with black pepper and the fried garlic.

1 lb. clams

½ cup dry white wine

6 hake or cod steaks, cut 1 inch thick through the bone

⅔ cup olive oil

4 garlic cloves, thinly sliced

¼ cup chopped fresh flatleaf parsley

sea salt and freshly ground black pepper

a cheesecloth-lined strainer

a heavy skillet or cazuela

SERVES 4–6

½ cup extra virgin olive oil

2 onions, halved and thinly sliced

2 garlic cloves, chopped

1–2 pinches of dried hot red pepper flakes

1 teaspoon crushed coriander seeds

½ teaspoon dried oregano

1½ lb. waxy potatoes, peeled and cut into wedges

2 bay leaves

5 tablespoons white wine or vermouth

½ teaspoon grated lemon peel

1½ lb. white fish (on or off the bone), cut into large chunks or steaks

2 small lemons, halved

1 tablespoon chopped fresh oregano

1 tablespoon chopped, fresh flatleaf parsley

sea salt and freshly ground black pepper

a large skillet or ovenproof skillet with a lid

a large ovenproof baking dish (optional)

SERVES 4

If you have a stovetop-to-oven pan, this dish can be cooked all in one pot. Use chunks of white fish such as monkfish, cod, sea bass, halibut, or haddock and choose potatoes that don't break up on cooking—large, waxy salad potatoes are ideal. As a general rule, yellow-fleshed potatoes are waxy, while white potatoes tend to be floury. Some steamed greens tossed in a little olive oil make a great accompaniment to this dish.

fish baked with lemon, oregano, and potatoes

Heat a large skillet or ovenproof skillet over medium heat and add the oil. Add the onion and fry for 2–3 minutes, then turn the heat down low. Add 1–2 pinches of salt, cover, and let the onion cook very gently for 10–12 minutes until soft and golden yellow. Add the garlic, red pepper flakes, crushed coriander seeds, and dried oregano. Cook for another 3–4 minutes.

Add the potatoes and bay leaves to the pan, turning them in the oily onions. Season with 1 teaspoon salt and several turns of the pepper mill, cook for a few minutes, then add the wine and lemon peel. When it bubbles, cover and cook gently for 15–20 minutes or until the potatoes are just tender.

Transfer the potatoes to a large ovenproof baking dish, if necessary. Season the fish with a little salt, then nestle the fish into the potatoes. Squeeze a little lemon juice from one of the lemon halves over the fish and spoon over a little of the oily juices. Add the lemon halves to the dish and turn in the oil.

Bake, uncovered, in a preheated oven at 400°F for 20–25 minutes, basting once or twice, until the potatoes are fully tender and the fish cooked through. The lemons should be touched with brown. Serve immediately, sprinkled with the fresh oregano and parsley.

meat and poultry

provençal roasted chicken with garlic, lemons, and olives

Free-range chicken, salty olives, and an intense lemon and garlic sauce make this French-style dish distinctive. Choose an olive oil which relates well to the olives and garlic: a lusty, green, fruity, Provençal oil would be perfect. You can also leave the lemon and garlic heads whole and serve a portion to each guest with a spoonful of the juice, rather than making the puréed sauce.

2½–3 lb. free-range chicken

3 tablespoons extra virgin olive oil

2 lemons

1 large bunch of fresh thyme

1 cup black olives, such as dry-cured Provençal

4 whole heads of garlic

½ cup full-bodied red wine (optional)

sea salt and freshly ground black pepper

SERVES 4

Pat the chicken dry with paper towels. Rub the skin with a little olive oil and sprinkle with salt inside and out. Put, breast side down, in a roasting pan.

Slice the lemons crosswise in a series of parallel slashes, but leave them attached at the base. Put half the thyme and one of the lemons inside the cavity and push more thyme between the trussed legs and underneath the bird. Push the olives under the bird. Add the remaining lemon to the pan.

Slice a "lid" off the top of each garlic head. Drizzle 1 teaspoon olive oil over each one and replace the lids. Brush the remaining oil over the chicken and lemon.

Roast the chicken, breast side down, in a preheated oven at 425°F for 40 minutes. Turn the bird on its back, put the prepared garlic heads underneath and roast for a further 35–40 minutes until deep golden brown. Prick the thigh at the thickest part—the juices should run a clear yellow. If there is any trace of pink, roast a little longer. Remove the chicken and olives from the pan. Let stand, covered, in a warm place for 8–10 minutes while you make the sauce (optional).

Pour off the pan juices from the pan. Measure 2 tablespoons of the stickiest, darkest juices and put in a food processor. Add the wine, if using. Press the soft, creamy centres out of the garlic heads and add to the food processor. Tip up the bird and let the juices run into the food processor. Add a quarter of the roasted lemon, pulled into pieces. Blend, in bursts, to a rich sauce. Taste and add extra stock if necessary. Gently simmer until the raw taste of wine has mellowed, about 3–5 minutes. Serve with the chicken.

chicken tagine with apricots

Many Moroccan dishes are seasoned with subtle spice combinations, mixed to order in the souk or bazaar. This chicken dish uses only four spices, two of which are used to rub into the skin of the chicken. If you can't find real saffron powder, double the amount of paprika and use half of that to help color the chicken. The apricots grow plump and juicy with blanching and give the chicken dish a good balance of sweet, salty, and sour flavors.

Mix the turmeric with the saffron, then rub it all over the chicken pieces. Put the apricots in a small saucepan, add 1 cup boiling water, bring very gently to a boil, cover with a lid, then simmer for about 10 minutes.

Heat the butter in a large flameproof casserole dish, then add the onions, and sauté for 5 minutes, stirring. Add the ginger, paprika, peppercorns, and salt. Put the chicken on top.

Add 1½ cups cold water to the apricots, then pour the apricots and their liquid over and around the chicken.

Add the parsley, bring to a boil, cover with a lid, then reduce to a simmer and cook, undisturbed, for 20 minutes. Add the apple. Simmer for a further 10–15 minutes, adding a little extra water if it looks too dry (the fruit absorbs much of the water).

Remove and discard the parsley. Serve the tagine with couscous or plain rice, topped with a few mint sprigs, if using.

½ teaspoon ground turmeric

½–1 teaspoon saffron powder

3 lb. chicken, cut into 8 or 10 pieces

8 oz. dried apricots

3 tablespoons butter or olive oil

2 onions, chopped

½ teaspoon ground ginger

½ teaspoon paprika

½ teaspoon crushed black peppercorns

1 teaspoon sea salt

a handful of fresh parsley, tied with twine

1 crisp apple, such as Granny Smith, cored but not peeled, then cut into 8 pieces

TO SERVE

fresh mint sprigs

couscous or plain rice

SERVES 4

3 lb. chicken, whole or quartered, or 4 breast or leg portions

2 tablespoons extra virgin olive oil

10 whole cloves

20 pearl onions or 10 shallots, halved

8 canned artichokes, drained

4 garlic cloves, chopped

2 tablespoons white wine vinegar or freshly squeezed lemon juice

⅓ cup rich tomato paste (double strength)

14-oz. can chopped tomatoes

24 black olives, such as Kalamata

a large bunch fresh or dried rosemary, oregano, thyme, or a mixture

2 tablespoons Greek Metaxa brandy (optional)

freshly ground black pepper

SERVES 4

In Greece stifado (or stifatho) can refer to a number of things, but essentially it is a thickened stew with tomato, garlic, and olive oil— perfect for winter. Sometimes made with beef or rabbit, guinea fowl, or even quail, it is easy to prepare and fragrant with herbs. The flambé is an unusual touch—entirely optional, but fun, especially if you use Metaxa brandy. Serve from the dish, accompanied with torn country bread, noodles, rice, or even chips.

greek chicken stifado

Pat the chicken dry with paper towels. Heat the olive oil in a large flameproof casserole dish, add the chicken, and sauté for 8–10 minutes, turning it from time to time.

Push the cloves into some of the onions and add them all to the pan. Add the artichokes, garlic, vinegar, tomato paste, tomatoes, olives, and freshly ground black pepper. Tuck in the herb sprigs around the edges.

Bring to a boil and reduce the heat to low. Cover and simmer for 30 minutes for chicken pieces, or about 60 minutes if using a whole bird, or until the chicken seems tender and the sauce has reduced and thickened.

Heat the brandy in a warmed ladle, if using, and pour it, flaming, over the stifado.

Note If you have access to a wine merchant who sells Greek wine, try the unusual mavrodaphne—sweet, red, and almost port-like.

Liver, along with other kinds of variety meats, has always been a delicacy in Mediterranean kitchens, especially in Greece, Italy, and Spain, where it can be served as a kabob, an appetizer, or an entrée. It is often cooked simply, with few spices or herbs. Lamb's liver, in small pieces, or halved chicken livers, are both appropriate for this recipe. Herb-flavored rice and seasonal greens, cooked then dressed with olive oil and a squeeze of lemon, are typical accompaniments.

chicken liver and bacon wraps

12 oz. chicken livers
or lamb's liver

1 nutmeg

8 slices thin, rindless streaky bacon, preferably smoked, halved lengthwise

2 tablespoons extra virgin olive oil

⅓ cup red wine or sweet red vermouth

¼ cup tomato purée

¼ cup chicken or lamb stock, or water

sea salt and freshly ground black pepper

toothpicks

SERVES 4

Use scissors to cut whole chicken livers into 2–4 pieces, discarding the membranous parts or any discolored areas. If using lamb's liver, cut it into ½-inch thick slices and then into 1-inch pieces. Pat the liver pieces dry with paper towels and dust with salt and pepper. Coarsely grate half the nutmeg and sprinkle over the liver, then wrap the bacon strips around each pair of liver pieces, using toothpicks to secure them.

Heat the olive oil in a large, nonstick skillet and sauté the liver and bacon wraps for 1½–2 minutes on each side or until the bacon fat is translucent, the liver golden, and the texture firm, but not hard. Push the meat to one side of the skillet.

Put the remaining nutmeg piece in the skillet with the wine, tomato purée, and stock. Cook, stirring over medium heat to dissolve the sediment on the base of the skillet, to make a sauce. Turn the liver briefly in the sauce and reheat gently for 1 minute, then serve.

This classic recipe originates from Andalucia, in southern Spain, where both ducks and olive groves are plentiful. Any variety of black or green olive will work here and they will taste even better if you pit them yourself.

duck with olives

Put the duck in a shallow dish, sprinkle with the thyme, sherry, salt, and pepper, and let marinate for about 30 minutes.

Pat the duck dry with paper towels and heat a skillet on high heat until smoking. Add the duck skin side down and fry without oil, on one side only, for 5 minutes until deep golden brown. Remove the duck to a plate. Drain off the duck fat and keep to cook potatoes on another occasion. Wipe the pan, heat 1 tablespoon of the olive oil, add the shallots, and fry until pale golden. Transfer to the plate with the duck.

Heat the remaining oil, add the onions and garlic, and fry gently for 5 minutes until softened but not colored. Increase the heat, add the wine, and bring to a boil. Transfer to a shallow ovenproof casserole dish, add the shallots and duck breasts, skin side up, and the marinade. Cook in a preheated oven at 425°F for 5–8 minutes. If you prefer the duck to be well done, cook for 3–5 minutes longer.

Add the olives and cook for a further 5 minutes. Slice the duck breasts lengthwise, then serve with the olive and onion mixture.

4 duck breasts, the fat scored into diamonds

4 sprigs of fresh thyme

2 tablespoons manzanilla sherry

3 tablespoons olive oil

10 shallots, separated into lobes

2 medium onions, finely chopped

3 garlic cloves, crushed

¼ cup dry white wine

20 black and 20 green olives, flesh sliced off the pits in 4 long pieces

sea salt and freshly ground black pepper

SERVES 4

4 cups dried lima beans, or
other white beans

1 lb. smoked Italian pancetta,
or slab bacon, in a piece

¼ cup olive oil

4 boneless duck breasts, halved
crosswise, or chicken legs
or thighs

1½ lb. fresh Toulouse sausages
or Italian coarse pork sausages,
cut into 3 pieces each

2 medium onions, chopped

1 large carrot, chopped

4-6 large garlic cloves, crushed

3 bay leaves

2 teaspoons dried thyme

2 whole cloves

3 tablespoons tomato paste

12 sun-dried tomatoes in oil,
drained and coarsely chopped

1½ cups fresh white
bread crumbs

4 tablespoons butter

sea salt and freshly ground
black pepper

SERVES 6–8

This hearty dish from southwest France is ideal for large gatherings on cold winter days. It is traditionally made with a type of haricot bean called lingot, but the creamy texture of lima beans also works well. All the components of the dish can be made days in advance, then assembled on the day. It reheats very well—simply top up with a little more liquid if it looks dry.

cassoulet

The night before, put the beans in a very large bowl, cover with plenty of cold water (to cover them by their depth again), and let soak for several hours or according to the package instructions.

The next day, drain the beans well and tip into a large saucepan. Cover with fresh water, bring to a boil, then simmer for about 1 hour or until just cooked. Drain well (reserving the cooking liquid).

Trim and discard the rind from the pancetta, and cut the flesh into large pieces. Heat 2 tablespoons of the olive oil in a skillet, brown the pieces in batches, and transfer to a plate. Heat the remaining oil in the skillet, add the duck breasts, and fry skin side down until the skin is golden. Transfer to the same plate as the pancetta. Brown the sausages in the same way and add to the plate. Add the onions to the skillet, then the carrot, garlic, bay leaves, dried thyme, cloves, tomato paste, and sun-dried tomatoes. Cook for 5 minutes until softening.

Put half the beans in a large, deep casserole dish. Add an even layer of all the meats, then the onion and tomato mixture. Season well with salt and pepper. Cover with the remaining beans, then add enough reserved hot cooking liquid so that the beans are almost covered. Sprinkle evenly with bread crumbs and dot with butter. Bake the cassoulet in a preheated oven at 350°F for about 1 hour until a golden crust has formed, then serve.

Souvlaki is the classic Greek kabob, a delicious combination of cubed lamb marinated in red wine with herbs and lemon juice. The meat is tenderized by the wine, resulting in a juicy and succulent dish.

souvlaki with bulghur wheat salad

Trim any large pieces of fat from the lamb and then cut the meat into 1-inch cubes. Put into a shallow, nonmetal dish. Add the rosemary, oregano, onion, garlic, wine, lemon juice, olive oil, salt, and pepper. Toss well, cover, and let marinate in the refrigerator for 4 hours. Return to room temperature for 1 hour before cooking.

To make the salad, soak the bulghur wheat in warm water for 30 minutes until the water has been absorbed and the grains have softened. Strain well to extract any excess water and transfer the wheat to a bowl. Add all the remaining ingredients, season with salt and pepper, to taste, and let rest for 30 minutes to develop the flavors.

Thread the lamb onto large rosemary stalks or metal skewers. Barbecue over hot coals for 10 minutes, or cook under a preheated broiler, turning and basting from time to time. Let rest for 5 minutes, then serve with the salad.

2 lb. boneless lamb, such as shoulder

1 tablespoon chopped, fresh rosemary

1 tablespoon dried oregano

1 onion, chopped

4 garlic cloves, chopped

1¼ cups red wine

freshly squeezed juice of 1 lemon

⅓ cup olive oil

sea salt and black pepper

BULGHUR WHEAT SALAD

3¼ cups bulghur wheat

1 cup chopped fresh parsley

½ cup fresh mint leaves

2 garlic cloves, crushed

½ cup extra virgin olive oil

freshly squeezed juice of 2 lemons

a pinch of caster sugar

sea salt and black pepper

6 large rosemary stalks or metal skewers

SERVES 6

Salsa Salmoretta is a spicy sauce from the Valencia and Alicante region of Spain and makes the perfect accompaniment to grilled lamb cutlets. Pork chops are equally delicious marinaded and cooked in this way.

lamb cutlets with salsa salmoretta

To marinate the cutlets, put the garlic, paprika, thyme sprigs and leaves, olive oil, salt, and pepper in a flat dish and stir to mix. Add the cutlets, turn to coat, and let marinate for 2 hours or overnight.

Heat a ridged stovetop grill pan until smoking, then add the cutlets and cook for 3 minutes on each side. Alternatively, barbecue over hot coals.

Meanwhile, to make the salsa salmoretta, put the shallot in a bowl and cover with cold water.

Cut a cross in the top of each tomato and put under a preheated hot broiler for 5 minutes, turning twice, until the skins are wrinkled and the flesh is soft. Peel, seed, and finely chop the flesh, then put in a bowl.

Meanwhile, crush the garlic, chili, and parsley to a paste with a mortar and pestle. Work in two-thirds of the chopped tomatoes. Drain the shallot and crush half of it with the tomatoes. Still stirring with the pestle, gradually add the oil to emulsify. Stir in the vinegar, the remaining tomatoes and shallot, salt, and pepper.

Serve the salsa with the cutlets.

3 garlic cloves, crushed

2 teaspoons sweet Spanish paprika (see page 65)

4 sprigs of fresh thyme (leaves picked off 2 of them)

3 tablespoons olive oil

12 lamb cutlets, trimmed

sea salt and freshly ground black pepper

SALSA SALMORETTA

1 large shallot, thinly sliced

3 ripe, medium tomatoes

2 garlic cloves, finely chopped

1 dried hot red chili, seeded and finely chopped

1 tablespoon finely chopped, fresh flatleaf parsley

⅓ cup olive oil

1½ teaspoons red wine vinegar

sea salt and freshly ground black pepper

a ridged stovetop grill pan (optional)

SERVES 4

STUFFING

3 tablespoons olive oil

2 large onions, finely chopped

2 lb. ground lamb

1 teaspoon ground allspice

1 teaspoon ground cinnamon

2 tablespoons pomegranate syrup or 2 tablespoons freshly squeezed lemon juice

⅔ cup hot water

3–4 tablespoons pine nuts, toasted in a dry skillet

4 tablespoons chopped fresh parsley

sea salt and freshly ground black pepper

KIBBEH

1½ cups fine bulghur wheat

1 large onion

2 lb. finely ground beef or lamb

1 teaspoon ground allspice

1 teaspoon ground cinnamon

6 tablespoons butter

sea salt and freshly ground black pepper

a selection of salads, to serve

a roasting pan, 12 x 10 x 2 inches, generously buttered

MAKES 12 PIECES

Kibbeh has an almost mythical status in Lebanese cooking. Before food processors appeared, it involved a lot of manual pounding, so it was mostly made for special occasions—not so now. Lebanese cooks decorate the top with intricate patterns before baking, but you can simply score it with a sharp knife to mark the portions.

baked kibbeh

To make the stuffing, heat the olive oil in a saucepan, add the onions, and sauté until they start to turn golden. Increase the heat, add the meat, and sauté until the moisture has evaporated and it starts to sizzle, 10–12 minutes. Add the allspice and cinnamon and fry for 2–3 minutes. Add salt, pepper, the pomegranate syrup, and hot water, then cover, and simmer for 30 minutes. Remove from the heat and stir in the pine nuts and parsley.

To make the kibbeh, soak the bulghur wheat in a bowl of cold water for 10 minutes. Change the water once and soak for another 5 minutes. Drain.

Put the onion in a food processor and pulse until finely chopped. Add the ground lamb, allspice, cinnamon, salt, and pepper. Process until smooth. Transfer to a bowl and add the drained bulghur wheat. Have a bowl of cold water with some ice cubes in it ready. Wet your hand in the cold water and knead the mixture for a few minutes. Divide the kibbeh mixture into 2 portions.

Dip your hands in the cold water, take a small handful from one of the kibbeh portions, flatten it between your palms, and spread it neatly at the base of the roasting pan. Continue, wetting your hands and joining the pieces neatly and overlapping slightly until the whole base is covered to about ½ inch thick.

Spread the stuffing evenly over the base. Use the other portion of kibbeh mixture to cover the top in the same way as before. Score the top with a sharp knife into diamond, rectangular, or square serving portions. Dot the butter over the top and bake in a preheated oven at 350°F for 20–30 minutes. (Do not overcook or it will become very dry.) Run a sharp knife around the edges, then cut the pieces carefully and lift individually onto a platter. Serve hot or at room temperature with a selection of salads.

moroccan butterflied and grilled lamb

Moroccan lamb is one of the best and easiest meat dishes for a big barbecue party. Butterflied lamb is just a leg of lamb that has been split open and the bones removed so that it is flat and an even thickness. A butcher can do this for you. After marinating, the leg can be cooked like one huge steak in much less time than cooking a whole leg, and is easy to carve for large numbers.

4-lb. leg of lamb, butterflied

1 tablespoon black peppercorns

1 tablespoon coriander seeds

1 tablespoon cumin seeds

1 tablespoon sweet Spanish paprika (see page 65)

2 teaspoon dried thyme

freshly squeezed juice of 1 lime

2 garlic cloves, crushed

½ cup plain yogurt

sea salt

TO SERVE

broiled flatbreads

salad

plain yogurt mixed with chopped fresh mint

SERVES 6–8

Trim any excess fat from the lamb and score the meat where necessary to make it the same thickness. Make deep slits all over the meat.

Put the peppercorns, coriander and cumin seeds, and paprika in a dry skillet, toast for a couple of minutes until aromatic, then grind or crush them. Transfer to a bowl, add the thyme, lime juice, garlic, yogurt, and salt to taste, then rub all over the cut side of the meat. Put in a shallow dish, cover, and let marinate in the refrigerator for at least 1 hour.

Grill the lamb skin side down over medium-hot coals for 10–12 minutes, then turn and cook for a further 10–12 minutes for medium rare. (For medium, cook for a total of 30–35 minutes; for well done, cook for a total of 40 minutes.)

Alternatively, cook the lamb on a foil-lined rack under a preheated medium-hot broiler for 20 minutes, then turn and continue for a further 20 minutes (the meat should be medium).

When cooked, remove from the heat, cover loosely with foil, and set aside in a warm place to rest for 10 minutes. Carve into long, thin slices. Serve with broiled flatbreads, salad, and minted yogurt.

luganega country sausage with lentils and wilted greens

Loukanika (Greece) and luganega (Italy) are similar types of sausage and have been known since antiquity. They contain fresh, coarse-cut pork and/or ground beef with salt, sugar, orange, chili, cumin or aniseed, and coriander, with plenty of garlic, red wine, and olive oil. This is all packed inside a long, traditional sausage casing and often sold coiled into a spiral. The sausages are then pan-fried, roasted, grilled, or broiled to a succulent golden brown. Buy them in Italian specialty shops, but if unavailable, you could substitute any dense, coarse-textured, spicy Italian link sausages. Avoid soft, mild, rusk-softened sausages as they are totally unsuited to this dish. Luganega also makes a great addition to the barbecue.

3 tablespoons extra virgin olive oil

1 lb. luganega coarse-cut spicy pork spiral

two 14-oz. cans Italian lentils, borlotti, cannellini, or lima beans

4 garlic cloves, chopped

1 onion, grated

1 lb. arugula or fresh flatleaf parsley, washed and shaken dry

2 tablespoons dry vermouth or white wine

sea salt and freshly ground black pepper

SERVES 4

Heat half the olive oil in a heavy skillet, add the sausage, and fry over medium heat for 6–8 minutes or until very hot, brown and firm. Drain and discard the liquid from the skillet. Keep the sausage hot over very low heat.

Meanwhile pour the lentils and their liquid into a saucepan and cook for 5 minutes or until very hot, then drain, discarding most of the liquid. Add salt, pepper, garlic, onion, and the remaining oil and stir over medium heat.

Put the arugula in the saucepan with the hot sausage. Add the vermouth and cook briefly, covered, until the leaves are vividly green and wilted. Serve the sausages on lentils with the wilted greens alongside or on top.

Meatballs, or polpette, in tomato sauce are an integral part of Italian food culture. When cooked, it is common practice to serve the sauce with pasta as an appetizer, followed by the meatballs and maybe a vegetable. If you make the meatballs very small, you can serve them in sauce with spaghetti. The meat can also be cooked as a polpettone—rolled into one large piece, and simmered for a couple of hours. In this case, the sauce is certainly used to dress pasta first and the meat is sliced and served as a separate course.

1 lb. shoulder or leg of pork

8-oz. piece unsmoked ham

8 oz. boneless pork chops, with fat

2 garlic cloves, crushed

2 tablespoon fennel seeds

a large pinch of hot red pepper flakes

2 teaspoons sea salt

1 tablespoon sugar

2 tablespoons coarsely crushed black pepper

olive oil, for frying

⅔ cup dry white wine

14-oz. can chopped tomatoes

½ cup tomato purée

sea salt and freshly ground black pepper

SERVES 6

pork and fennel meatballs in tomato sauce

Trim the shoulder of pork, ham, and pork chops of any skin or connective tissue. Cut the meat into large chunks, then pass them through the coarse blade of an electric mincer or chop very finely with a large sharp knife or cleaver (do not use a food processor).

Put the meat in a large bowl, add the garlic, fennel seeds, red pepper flakes, salt, sugar, and pepper. Mix with clean hands or a large wooden spoon. At this stage, the sausage meat is ready to use, but you can cover the bowl and let it mature in the refrigerator overnight.

With dampened hands, shape into meatballs about the size of a walnut. To cook, heat 2 tablespoons of the olive oil in a skillet and quickly brown the meatballs all over, in batches if necessary. Remove to a plate with a slotted spoon and add the wine. Deglaze the pan and let the wine bubble until there is only 1 tablespoon left. Add the canned tomatoes and tomato purée, salt, and pepper. Bring back to a boil, then return the meatballs to the sauce. Partially cover with a lid and simmer for 30–40 minutes, topping up with water if the sauce is becoming too dry. Serve as it is or dress pasta with the sauce as an appetizer and eat the meatballs as a course on their own (see recipe introduction).

This recipe, modeled on veal escalopes with Marsala, is easy to make with pork tenderloins, cut into small oval escalopes or scaloppine. Serve with side dishes such as buttered spinach or tiny roasted potatoes, and a glass of the same Marsala used in the sauce.

pork tenderloin with marsala

Cut the tenderloin crosswise into ½-inch slices. Cut each slice almost through again, then open out, and press flat with the heel of your palm. You should have about 24 flattened, butterflied pieces or scaloppine.

Sift the flour, salt, and ginger together onto a flat plate. Press 6 pieces of pork into this mixture until well coated on both sides.

Put half the butter and half the olive oil in a nonstick skillet and heat until sizzling. Cook the almonds briefly until golden, then remove with a slotted spoon, and set aside. Add 6 of the prepared scaloppine to the skillet and cook for 2 minutes each side, pressing them down well, then use tongs to remove, and keep hot. Continue with a second batch of 6.

Add half the Marsala to the skillet and stir to dissolve the sediment. Pour off into a bowl and keep it warm. Wash and dry the skillet.

Using the remaining butter and oil, repeat the process until the second batch of pork is cooked. Keep hot in the same way.

Pour the remaining Marsala into the skillet, then add the jellied meat stock or consommé. Scrape, stir, and heat until well dissolved, then add the reserved warm skillet sauce made earlier. Heat again until sticky and intensely flavored. Return the pork to the skillet and turn it in the hot sauce.

Serve 6 scaloppine per person, with a spoonful of Marsala glaze and the almonds.

1½–2 pork tenderloins, about 1½ lb.

⅔ cup all-purpose flour

1 teaspoon salt

1 teaspoon ground ginger or freshly grated nutmeg

4 tablespoons salted butter

2 tablespoons extra virgin olive oil

¼ cup blanched almonds, flaked or whole

½ cup sweet Marsala wine

2 tablespoons jellied veal or beef stock, or canned beef or chicken consommé

SERVES 4

osso buco with gremolata

*The Italian name for this dish means "bone with a hole."
For the last 1 1/2 hours of cooking, you can cook this in
the oven at 350°F instead of on the stove, but make
sure the casserole dish is flameproof. Gremolata is the
traditional accompaniment for osso buco and should
be made at the last minute to preserve its herby zing.*

Dust the veal shanks with flour. Heat the olive oil in a large
saucepan, add the veal, and fry over medium-low heat for a
few minutes, until brown. Remove from the pan and set aside.

Add a little more oil to the pan if needed, heat, and add the
garlic, onions, and celery. Cook for 5 minutes until soft but not
brown. Add the tomato purée and tomatoes, mix well, and add
the wine, stock, and salt and pepper to taste. Return the meat
to the pan and gently bring to a boil. Cover with a lid and
simmer gently for 1 1/2 hours, adding a little more stock or wine
from time to time if needed. Let cool, cover, and chill.

When ready to serve, put the osso buco in a preheated oven
at 350°F until simmering, then continue cooking for 15 minutes
or until heated right through.

Meanwhile, to make the gremolata, put the lemon peel, garlic,
and parsley into a bowl and stir well.

Remove the osso buco from the oven and serve topped with
the gremolata and with mashed potato and green beans.

8 veal shank cross cuts with the
marrow bone, 10 oz. each

1/4 cup all-purpose flour

1/4 cup olive oil

3 garlic cloves, crushed
and chopped

2 onions, chopped

4 celery ribs, chopped

1 tablespoon tomato paste

two 14-oz. cans
chopped tomatoes

1 cup dry white wine

1 1/4 cups vegetable stock

sea salt and freshly ground
black pepper

GREMOLATA

finely grated peel of 3 lemons

3 garlic cloves, finely chopped

a large bunch of fresh flatleaf
parsley, finely chopped

TO SERVE

mashed potato

steamed green beans

SERVES 8

Spanish fries are the traditional accompaniment for these succulent steaks and are extremely tasty due to the olive oil they are fried in. Pimientos de Padrón are another classic accompaniment, although they can be rather hot!

pan-grilled steaks with olive sauce

4 rib eye steaks, 1 inch thick

3 garlic cloves, crushed

3 tablespoons finely chopped, fresh flatleaf parsley

⅓ cup extra virgin olive oil

freshly squeezed juice of 1 lemon

sea salt and freshly ground black pepper

Spanish fries, to serve*

OLIVE SAUCE

¼ cup olive oil

1 tablespoon sherry vinegar

4 oz. mixed pitted green and black olives

2 garlic cloves, crushed

2 firm tomatoes, peeled, seeded, and finely chopped

sea salt and freshly ground black pepper

a ridged stovetop grill pan

SERVES 4

Put the steaks in a flat dish, sprinkle with the garlic, black pepper, and half the parsley, pour over the olive oil and lemon juice, and rub in. Set aside for 2 hours or overnight in the refrigerator. Remove from the refrigerator 30 minutes before cooking and sprinkle with salt.

Meanwhile, to make the olive sauce, put the olive oil in a bowl and whisk in the sherry vinegar. Put the olives in a food processor and blend to chop into small, evenly sized bits (not a purée). Put in the bowl with the oil mixture, add the rest of the ingredients, and season lightly with salt and pepper.

When ready to cook the steak, heat a ridged stovetop grill pan over high heat. When smoking, add the steaks, and cook for 1½ minutes on each side for rare, 2 minutes for medium, and 2½–3 minutes for well done. Alternatively, cook on the barbecue. Sprinkle with the rest of the parsley and serve with the sauce and Spanish fries and pimientos de Padrón, if liked.

*Note To make Spanish fries, cut 1½ lb. potatoes, such as Belle de Fontenay, into ¼-inch slices, then into ¼-inch fingers. Rinse well in cold water to remove the starch, then pat dry on paper towels.

Fill a deep-fryer with pure olive oil to the manufacturer's recommended level and heat to 350°F. Working in batches, fry the potatoes until golden, then drain on paper towels and keep hot.

2 lb. beef, such as shoulder or topside, cut into ½-inch thick slices

¼ cup extra virgin olive oil

4 garlic cloves, sliced

1 cup thick-cut unsmoked bacon, cut in small dice, or bacon lardons, cubed

3 carrots, halved lengthwise

12–16 baby onions, peeled

6 plum tomatoes, peeled, then thickly sliced

peel of 1 orange, removed in one piece

1 bunch of fresh herbs, such as parsley, thyme, bay leaf, and rosemary, tied with twine

½ cup walnut halves

1 cup robust red wine

2 tablespoons Cognac or brandy

¾ cup beef stock or water

6-inch square of pork or bacon rind (optional)

chopped flatleaf parsley, to serve

SERVES 4–6

This warming beef stew is a classic dish from the south of France. Rich with red wine, baby onions, and orange peel, it can be served absolutely plain, or with accompaniments such as pasta, mashed potatoes, or rice.

boeuf en daube

Cut the beef into 2½-inch squares. Heat the olive oil in a large flameproof casserole dish and sauté the garlic, bacon, carrots, and onions for about 4–5 minutes or until aromatic. Remove from the dish. Put a layer of meat in the bottom of the dish, then add half the sautéed vegetable mixture and a second layer of meat. Add the remaining vegetable mixture, the tomatoes, orange peel, bundle of herbs, and walnuts.

Put the wine into a small saucepan and bring to a boil. Add the Cognac or brandy and warm for a few seconds, shaking the pan a little, to let the alcohol cook away. Pour the hot liquids over the meat with just enough stock so that it's barely covered. Put the pork rind, if using, on top.

Heat the casserole until simmering, then cover with aluminum foil and a lid, and simmer gently for 2 hours or until the meat is tender and the juices rich and sticky.

The dish can also be cooked in the oven. Just bring to a boil over high heat, reduce to a simmer, cover with foil, replace the lid, and cook in the oven at 300°F for 2½ hours or until very tender.

Remove and discard the rind: it will have given a velvety quality to the sauce. Sprinkle with parsley and serve hot.

meat roll simmered in tomato sauce

*A traditional recipe from the Naples area, in which a lean piece
of beef is rolled around a savory stuffing and slowly cooked in
a tomato and vegetable sauce. The sauce is usually served tossed
with pasta as an appetizer, the meat served as the entrée with just a
little sauce, followed by a salad or a plate of green vegetables.*

Soak the bread crumbs in a little water. Soak the currants in lukewarm water for
15 minutes, then drain. Put the beef between 2 sheets of plastic wrap and beat
out with a meat mallet or rolling pin to flatten slightly, to about ¼ inch thick.
Season with salt and pepper.

Lightly squeeze out the soaked bread crumbs and put in a bowl. Add ⅔ of the
chopped prosciutto, the parsley, garlic, marjoram, and egg yolks, season with salt
and pepper and mix well. Spread this mixture over the beef and sprinkle with the
drained currants and the pine nuts. Roll up the beef, tucking in the sides, and tie
up with fine twine.

Heat the olive oil in the casserole dish on top of the stove, add the rolled beef,
and brown it all over. Transfer to a plate. Add the remaining prosciutto, the
clove, onion, carrot, and celery to the dish and cook for 10 minutes until the
vegetables are soft. Stir in the tomato paste and 1 generous cup warm water.

Return the rolled beef to the dish and bring to a boil. Cover with a piece of
waxed paper just big enough to fit inside your casserole dish. Cover with the lid,
then transfer to a preheated oven at 350°F for about 2 hours, adding a little
extra water every now and then. When cooked, lift the beef out onto a warm
plate, cover, and set aside.

Pour the contents of the dish into a food processor and work to a purée. Reheat
and taste for seasoning. To serve, slice the beef thickly and serve with a little
sauce ladled over. Pass the remaining sauce around separately, or use for pasta.

2½ cups fresh bread crumbs

1 tablespoon currants

1 slice lean rump steak, 1 lb.,
about ½ inch thick

6 oz. prosciutto, finely chopped

⅓ cup chopped fresh
flatleaf parsley

1 garlic clove, finely chopped

½ teaspoon dried marjoram

2 egg yolks

1 tablespoon pine nuts

2 tablespoons olive oil

1 whole clove

1 small onion, finely chopped

1 small carrot, finely chopped

1 celery rib, finely chopped

2 tablespoons tomato paste

sea salt and freshly ground
black pepper

SERVES 4

vegetables

⅔ cup extra virgin olive oil

3 medium eggplants, rinsed and halved lengthwise

sea salt and freshly ground black pepper

STUFFING

2 onions, finely chopped

4 garlic cloves, finely chopped

1 teaspoon ground cumin

1 lb. ripe tomatoes, chopped

1 tablespoon dried oregano

½ teaspoon sugar

3 tablespoons chopped fresh flatleaf parsley

1 tablespoon tomato paste, diluted with ⅔ cup hot water

sea salt and freshly ground black pepper

SERVES 6

This is a dish full of summer flavors. It can be served hot as an entrée or as part of a mixed meze as it is equally good served at room temperature. It derives its Turkish name, Imam Bayildi, from an old fable about the Turkish priest—the Imam—who fainted either from overindulging in this rich dish or from meanness because of the extravagant amount of olive oil used.

baked eggplants with garlic and tomatoes

Heat half the olive oil in a large skillet, add 3 pieces of eggplant, and shallow-fry, turning them over until light golden on both sides, 10–15 minutes. Remove and rest on paper towels. Repeat with the remaining 3 pieces. Arrange the pieces side by side in an ovenproof dish and season with salt and pepper.

To make the stuffing, heat the remaining olive oil in a saucepan, add the onions, and sauté gently until they start to color. Add the garlic and cumin, fry for 2–3 minutes, then add the tomatoes, oregano, salt, pepper, sugar, and ⅔ cup water. Cover and cook for 15 minutes, stirring occasionally.

Stir in the parsley, then divide the stuffing into 6 equal portions. Pile each portion along the length of each eggplant half. Add the diluted tomato paste to the dish and cook in a preheated oven 375°F for 45 minutes, basting the eggplants once during cooking. Serve hot or at room temperature.

ratatouille

Originally from Nice, ratatouille is one of those reliable recipes that just gets better as it matures. It can be served with many dishes, and also by itself with lots of crusty bread. Don't use green bell peppers as they are too bitter.

Cut the eggplants into large, bite-size pieces, put them in a colander, sprinkle well with salt, and let drain for 1 hour. Cut the peppers in half, remove the white membrane and seeds, and slice the flesh into thick strips.

Heat the olive oil in a flameproof casserole dish and fry the onions, garlic, and coriander seeds until soft and transparent, but not colored. Add the wine and boil to reduce.

Meanwhile, rinse and drain the eggplants and dry on paper towels. Add the bell peppers and eggplants to the dish and cook for about 10 minutes, stirring occasionally until softening around the edges, but not browning. Add the tomatoes, sugar, and olives. Heat to simmering point, season well with salt and pepper, then partially cover with a lid and cook for about 25 minutes. Add the parsley, if using, and serve hot or cold.

2 eggplants

3 bell peppers (red, yellow, or orange)

3 tablespoons olive oil

2 large onions, thinly sliced

2 garlic cloves, crushed

2 teaspoons finely crushed coriander seeds

5 tablespoons white wine

14-oz. can chopped tomatoes

1 teaspoon sugar

about 20 Greek-style dry-cured black olives

sea salt and freshly ground black pepper

parsley leaves, to serve (optional)

SERVES 6

This is a great dish for vegetarians and carnivores alike. Flavored with fresh mint and sesame seeds, and topped with spicy harissa sauce, the couscous goes well with any roast meat or vegetable dish. Morrocan Mint Tea (page 234) is delicious to drink after this dish.

sesame and mint couscous with winter vegetables

2 tablespoons unsalted butter

2 garlic cloves, crushed

1 tablespoon sweet Spanish paprika (see page 65)

2 teaspoons cumin

½ teaspoon ground ginger

1 teaspoon sea salt

1 teaspoon freshly ground black pepper

2 bay leaves

2 tablespoons tomato paste

14-oz. can chopped tomatoes

2 whole fresh green chilies

2 large carrots, peeled and cut into wedges

2 large parsnips, peeled and cut into wedges

1 lb. potatoes, peeled and cut into 2-inch chunks

2 large zucchini, cut into wedges

8 oz. butternut squash or pumpkin, peeled, seeded, and cut into 2-inch chunks

2 tablespoons harissa paste mixed with ½ cup hot water, to serve

SESAME AND MINT COUSCOUS

2 cups instant couscous

2 cups boiling water

1 stick butter, cubed

4 tablespoons chopped fresh mint

3 tablespoons toasted sesame seeds

sea salt and freshly ground black pepper

SERVES 6

Melt the butter in a heavy casserole dish, add the garlic, and cook for 1 minute over medium heat. Add the paprika, cumin, ginger, salt, pepper, bay leaves, tomato paste, and tomatoes, and stir well. Bring to a boil, then add the chilies, carrots, and parsnips.

Pour in enough water to cover (about 1¾ cups), then return to a boil, partially cover with a lid, and simmer gently for 20 minutes. Add the potatoes, zucchini, and butternut squash, pushing them under the liquid, and cook for a further 20 minutes or until the potatoes are tender. Take care not to overcook the vegetables or they will disintegrate.

Meanwhile, make the sesame and mint couscous. Put the couscous in a bowl and pour the boiling water into a measuring jug, stir in the butter and mint, then pour evenly over the couscous. Cover tightly with plastic wrap and let stand for 5 minutes.

Uncover the couscous and fluff up the grains with a fork. Stir in the sesame seeds, then taste and season well with salt and pepper. Pile the couscous onto a large serving platter, then make a hollow in the center and heap the spicy vegetable stew into the middle. Serve immediately with the harissa paste mixture in a small bowl.

provençal vegetable tian

1 small eggplant, cut into
½-inch cubes

2 teaspoons salt

2 tablespoons extra virgin
olive oil

2 tablespoons butter

4 garlic cloves, chopped

1 onion, sliced

4 scallions or 1 baby
leek, sliced

a handful of spinach or Swiss
chard, chopped

a handful of baby asparagus
or green beans, cut into
1-inch lengths

8 large eggs

1 cup crème fraîche or
sour cream

1 cup grated Parmesan,
pecorino, or Gruyère cheese

SERVES 4

A tian is a shallow baking dish, often glazed earthenware. Like the word "casserole," the name has also come to mean the food cooked in it. Tians usually contain vegetables and herbs and sometimes cheese and eggs, or even a little rice or petit salé bacon. It can be served in spoonfuls or in wedges, with bread or a salad.

Put the eggplant in a plastic or ceramic dish, sprinkle with the salt, and set aside for 15 minutes or until all the other ingredients have been prepared.

Heat the olive oil and 1 tablespoon of the butter in a skillet, add the garlic, onion, scallions, spinach, and asparagus and sauté over medium heat for 6–8 minutes, stirring constantly, until the vegetables are soft but still colorful. Remove with a slotted spoon.

Put the eggplant cubes in a colander and let drain—do not wash them. Pat them dry with paper towels, removing most of the salt. Add the remaining butter and the eggplant to the skillet, and sauté for 5 minutes.

Put the eggs, crème fraîche, and Parmesan in a bowl and beat with a fork.

Transfer the eggplant, vegetables, and their juices and oil into a casserole dish, distributing them evenly. Pour the egg and cheese mixture over the top and bake in a preheated oven at 400°F for 5 minutes. Reduce the heat to 350°F for a further 20 minutes and cook until set and nicely brown.

Serve hot, warm, or cool.

Pastries are at the heart of Greek food and culture and each village and every island has its own indigenous versions. This sensational pie, known as spanakotyropitta, is the most common and most delicious kind. It can be served as an entrée with rice or salad, or cut into small squares and served as a meze dish.

spinach and cheese pie

1 packet phyllo dough,
16 oz., thawed if frozen

9 tablespoons butter, melted

FILLING

1 lb. fresh leaf spinach, rinsed

¼ cup extra virgin olive oil

1 large onion, finely chopped

4–5 scallions, trimmed
and coarsely chopped

4 eggs

8 oz. feta cheese

3 oz. fresh dill, finely chopped

3–4 tablespoons finely chopped
fresh flatleaf parsley

¼ cup milk

sea salt and freshly
ground black pepper

a roasting pan, 13 x 9 inches

MAKES ABOUT 12 PIECES

To make the filling, put the spinach in a large saucepan of water, cover, and cook gently, stirring occasionally, for 5–6 minutes until wilted. Drain the spinach thoroughly in a colander. Wipe the saucepan dry, add the olive oil, and sauté the onion and scallions until translucent. Add the spinach, salt, and pepper and sauté for 4–5 minutes. Let cool a little. Beat the eggs in a large bowl, crumble in the cheese, add the herbs, milk, and spinach, and mix well with a fork.

Unroll the dough carefully—you will have an oblong stack of paper-thin sheets. Brush the roasting pan with the hot melted butter. Then butter sparingly the top sheet of pastry and lay it into the pan, folding any excess on one side (keep in mind that the pastry will shrink when cooked). Continue the same way folding the excess on alternate ends until you have used about half the pastry. Add the filling and spread it evenly. Fold the sides over it and start covering with the remaining pastry sheets, brushing each one with the melted butter. Try to be as neat as possible.

Finally, brush the top layer of pastry generously with butter. Using a sharp knife, score the top layers of pastry into diamond or square shapes—do it carefully to avoid spilling the filling. Using your fingertips, sprinkle a little cold water on top to stop the pastry curling.

Bake in a preheated oven at 375°F for 50 minutes until golden on top. (It is nice to have it still a little moist in the center.) Slice carefully all the way to the bottom sheets of pastry and serve hot or at room temperature.

bell peppers stuffed with caperberries

4 red or yellow bell peppers, quartered lengthwise and seeded

16 canned anchovy fillets, rinsed and drained

16 caperberries or 2 tablespoons capers, rinsed and drained

a small bunch of marjoram or oregano, chopped

2 tablespoons extra virgin olive oil

freshly ground black pepper

SERVES 4

Bell peppers are ubiquitous ingredients in Italian antipasti and respond well to broiling and roasting which develops the natural sugars. With salty anchovies and sharp pickled caperberries or capers, they really come into their own in this elegant dish from southern Italy.

Arrange the pepper quarters in a large roasting dish or pan.

Using scissors or a small knife, cut each anchovy fillet lengthwise into 2 strips. Put 2 strips into each pepper segment. Add a caperberry or a share of the capers to each segment and sprinkle with the chopped herbs and olive oil.

Roast, uncovered, towards the top of a preheated oven at 350°F for 20–30 minutes or until wrinkled, aromatic, and beginning to blacken a little at the edges. Serve hot, warm, or cool, sprinkled with black pepper.

This Spanish dish of summer or fall vegetables roasted to sweetness is deceptively simple and its success depends on good olive oil and vegetables cooked in their skins for extra flavor. There are many Mediterranean variations and in some parts of France and Spain, you will find anchovy strips lining the pepper halves, or fragments of salt cod, and sometimes capers, olives, or even cubes of goat cheese. Different herbs can be added just before serving and even a few drops of vinegar, but on the whole simplicity is best. Serve as an accompaniment or as an entrée with bread.

spanish roasted vegetables

Leave the stems on the bell peppers, but remove and discard the pith and seeds. Cut the onions almost in half crosswise, leaving one side joined. Remove and discard the seeds and pith from the squash, but leave otherwise intact.

Cut the unpeeled heads of garlic almost in half crosswise, leaving a hinge of papery skin. Pour a teaspoon of the olive oil over the cut surfaces of the garlic, then put the bulbs back together again. Wrap up in foil, to make 2 packets.

Arrange all the prepared vegetables, eggplants included, in a single layer in 1 or 2 roasting pans, cut sides uppermost. Sprinkle with 3–4 tablespoons of the oil.

Roast in a preheated oven at 475°F for 35–40 minutes or until soft and fragrant. Transfer to a serving dish, and sprinkle with black pepper and the herbs and remaining oil. Serve hot or warm.

2 red bell peppers, halved lengthwise

2 yellow or orange bell peppers, halved lengthwise

2 red onions, unpeeled

4 slices butternut squash or pumpkin, about ½ inch thick, seeded if necessary, or 2 large zucchini, halved lengthwise, scored with a fork

2 baby eggplants or 1 large, sliced lengthwise and scored with a fork

2 whole garlic heads

6–8 tablespoons extra virgin olive oil

freshly ground black pepper

a small handful of fresh herbs, such as parsley, oregano, mint, and thyme

SERVES 4

artichokes provençal

Based on a Provençal dish, this is a delicious vegetable stew flavored with lovage and thyme. Only a small amount of lovage is needed to give maximum flavor. If you've never tasted it, prepare to be smitten—it's a delightful herb, full of character, similar to celery in some ways. Baby artichokes are picked before the hairy choke has formed and can be cooked and eaten whole.

Squeeze the cut lemon halves into a bowl of cold water and add the lemon skins. Set aside to add the artichokes as they are prepared (the acidulated water will prevent them from discoloring).

To prepare the artichokes, remove about 3 layers of tough leaves from the outside, cut off the top ½ inch of the leaves, and trim the stalks to about 1 inch. Using a vegetable peeler, peel the stalks. As you work, add the artichokes to the bowl of lemon water.

Heat 1 tablespoon of oil in a flameproof casserole dish, add the bacon, and fry until crisp and golden. Transfer to a plate.

Add the remaining olive oil to the casserole dish, then fry the whole shallots and garlic until golden. Drain the artichokes and add to the pan. Add the carrots and stir-fry for 2 minutes. Add the wine, bring to a boil, and reduce for 2 minutes. Add the stock and simmer for 2 minutes, then add the lovage, thyme, salt, and pepper.

Cover and cook in a preheated oven at 400°F for 20 minutes until the artichokes are tender. Add the beans, return to the oven, and heat through, uncovered, for 5 minutes. Serve with bread, boiled rice, and salad.

1 lemon, halved

18–24 baby artichokes, depending on size

3 tablespoons extra virgin olive oil

7 oz. smoked bacon pieces (lardons) or 6 slices bacon, cut into strips

10 oz. small shallots

3 garlic cloves, halved

4 carrots, halved lengthwise and cut into fine strips

¾ cup white wine

½ cup vegetable stock

2 young sprigs of lovage, or a few celery leaves

a large sprig of thyme

1 cup cooked white beans, such as cannellini beans

sea salt and freshly ground black pepper

TO SERVE

crusty bread

boiled rice, preferably red Camargue

salad greens

SERVES 6

The natural sugars in the vegetables are used in this Neapolitan dish to caramelize and combine with the vinegar, giving it its characteristic flavor. It is traditionally done quickly in a skillet, but when cooking in quantity, it is easier to roast the vegetables in the oven.

sweet and sour carrots and zucchini with mint

2 medium zucchini

2 medium carrots

⅓ cup extra virgin olive oil

a few sprigs of mint, plus extra to serve

2 tablespoons wine vinegar

sea salt and freshly ground black pepper

SERVES 4

Top and tail the zucchini and carrots and cut into matchsticks the size of your little finger. Put half the olive oil in a bowl, add the carrots, and toss to coat. Transfer the carrots to a roasting pan and cook in a preheated oven at 400°F for 15 minutes.

Meanwhile, toss the zucchini in the remaining olive oil, then stir into the carrots when they have cooked for 15 minutes. Roast together for a further 10 minutes until tender and caramelized. Remove from the oven, season with salt and pepper, then add the mint and vinegar to the roasting pan, mixing well.

Set the pan over high heat on top of the stove and let it bubble for a few seconds to reduce the vinegar. Mix well. Serve hot or at room temperature with extra mint.

⅓ cup dried currants
or golden raisins

12 saffron threads or 1 small
package saffron powder

1 medium cauliflower,
about 2 lb.

¼ cup olive oil

1 onion, thinly sliced
or finely chopped

2 garlic cloves, finely chopped

6 anchovy fillets in oil,
rinsed and coarsely chopped,
or 3 salted anchovies,
boned, rinsed, and chopped

sea salt and freshly
ground black pepper

a handful of fresh basil leaves,
to serve

BREAD CRUMBS

¼ cup olive oil

1 whole garlic clove,
peeled and lightly
bruised to crack open

¼ cup dry or fresh bread crumbs

SERVES 4

This dish originates from Sicily where there are several varieties of cauliflower, namely unblanched green cauliflower, blanched white cauliflower, and a curious lime green variety with pointed florets—all of which can be cooked in the same way.

cauliflower with saffron and toasted bread crumbs

To make the bread crumbs, heat the olive oil in a skillet, add the garlic clove, fry gently until lightly brown, then remove it from the skillet. Stir in the bread crumbs and cook over medium heat, stirring constantly, for 2 minutes until golden. Immediately, pour into a strainer set over a bowl to drain. Let cool.

Put the currants in a small bowl and pour over boiling water to cover. Let soak for 20 minutes. Put the saffron in a cup, add 3 tablespoons warm water, and leave to infuse for 15–20 minutes. Remove the leaves and tough stalk from the cauliflower and divide the head into large florets. Cook for just 5 minutes in boiling salted water. Drain, reserving ⅔ cup of the cooking water.

Heat the olive oil in a deep skillet and gently fry the onion and garlic for about 5 minutes until soft and golden. Stir in the anchovies and the drained currants and cook for 3 minutes until the anchovies dissolve. Add the saffron and its water, the drained cauliflower, and the reserved cauliflower water. Stir well, then heat to a slow simmer. Season with pepper only. Partially cover with a lid and cook for 5 minutes until the cauliflower is tender. Serve sprinkled with the bread crumbs and a few torn basil leaves.

whole onions
baked in their skins

In Sicily, onions are roasted in huge metal trays, then put on display outside vegetable shops. Sicilians love the sweetness of onions cooked like this. Normally the onions are simply squeezed out of their skins after roasting, but they also taste good finished off with a sweet and sour sauce.

Trim the root end of each onion so that they will stand up securely. Rub with olive oil. Cut a deep cross in the top of each one, slicing towards the base so that it is cut almost into quarters.

Pack the onions closely together in a flameproof casserole dish or roasting pan. Sprinkle with olive oil, salt, and pepper. Bake in a preheated oven at 375°F for 1–1¼ hours until they are tender in the center.

Lift out the onions onto a serving dish, leaving the juices behind. Set the roasting pan over medium heat and add the wine, vinegar, golden raisins, fennel seeds, and capers. Scrape up any sediment and boil for a couple of minutes until reduced and syrupy.

Taste, add salt and pepper if necessary, then pour the sauce over the onions.

6 large white or red onions

⅔ cup white wine

3 tablespoons red wine vinegar

2 tablespoons golden raisins

1 teaspoon fennel seeds

1 tablespoon small salted capers, rinsed

sea salt and freshly ground black pepper

olive oil, for basting and serving

SERVES 6

With its lush intriguing taste, okra is the beloved vegetable of the Eastern Mediterranean. This vegetarian okra dish can be cooked well in advance and will wait happily at a meze table. The dried limes, which can be obtained from Arab or Indian stores, add an altogether new dimension to its sweet taste.

okra with dried limes

2 lb. fresh okra

⅔ cup extra virgin olive oil

1 large onion, sliced

1 teaspoon ground coriander

½ teaspoon ground allspice

1¾ lb. fresh tomatoes, sliced, or 14-oz. can tomatoes

2 dried limes (optional)

½ teaspoon sugar

2 tablespoons finely chopped cilantro

sea salt and freshly ground black pepper

SERVES 6

To prepare the okra, pare the conical tops with a sharp knife (similar to peeling potatoes). Put them in a bowl, cover with cold water briefly, then drain —handle with care.

Heat the olive oil in a wide saucepan, add the onion, and sauté until light golden. Add the ground coriander and allspice, then when aromatic, add the tomatoes, dried limes, if using, sugar, salt, and pepper. Cook for 10 minutes, pressing the limes with a spatula to extract their sour juices.

Add the okra and spread them evenly in the pan. Pour in enough hot water until they are almost immersed in the sauce.

Cook gently for about 30 minutes—shake the pan occasionally but don't stir as okra is fragile. Sprinkle the cilantro over the top and simmer for 5-10 minutes more. Serve the dish warm or at room temperature.

2 cups shelled fava beans,
fresh or frozen and thawed,
(1½ lb. before shelling)

4 tablespoons olive oil

8 oz. scallions,
coarsely chopped

1¼ cups vegetable stock
or water

4 fresh, canned, or frozen
artichoke hearts, quartered

2 cups shelled peas,
fresh or frozen and thawed
(1 lb. before shelling)

a large pinch of sugar

2 tablespoons chopped
fresh mint

sea salt and freshly
ground black pepper

SERVES 4

This exquisite medley of green vegetables from western Sicily is one of the best ways to use sweet garden peas, fava beans, and artichokes. Fava beans taste much better if popped out of their skins to reveal the bright green tender bean. This dish is often served as a soup, or you can add creamy ricotta to make a light lunch.

sicilian green vegetables

Bring a large saucepan of salted water to a boil, add the fava beans, and boil for 1 minute. Drain and plunge them into a bowl of cold water to cool them quickly and set the color. Nick the skin at the top of a bean and gently squeeze at the bottom to pop it out. Continue until all are done.

Heat the olive oil, add the scallions, and cook over gentle heat for a couple of minutes until they wilt and soften, but do not let brown. Add the stock and season well with salt and pepper. Bring to a boil, then reduce the heat, and simmer for 5 minutes.

Add the peas and cook for a further 5 minutes, then gently stir in the beans and the artichoke hearts. Simmer for another 3–4 minutes. Remove from the heat and add sugar to taste, then stir in the mint. Let cool so the flavors will develop. Serve at room temperature.

2½ lb. fresh spinach

½ cup extra virgin olive oil

4 anchovy fillets in oil,
drained and chopped

3 tablespoons chopped fresh
flatleaf parsley

3 tablespoons dried currants or
small raisins, soaked in
warm water for 15 minutes

¼ cup pine nuts

freshly grated nutmeg

sea salt and freshly
ground black pepper

SERVES 4

This specialty of Genoa in Liguria uses anchovies as a way of adding saltiness, giving the earthy spinach a depth it would not have otherwise. The combination of salt (anchovies) and sweet (dried fruit), coupled with mild, creamy pine nuts in savory dishes is common all over Italy.

spinach with anchovies and pine nuts

Tear the stems off the spinach, discard the stems, and wash the leaves very well in plenty of cold water to remove any grit and sand. Shake dry in a colander or salad spinner, but leave some water clinging to the leaves.

Put the leaves in a covered saucepan and cook for a few minutes until they wilt. Drain in a colander but do not squeeze dry—you need large pieces of spinach.

Warm the olive oil in a large skillet, add the chopped anchovies and parsley, and stir for 2–3 minutes over medium heat until the anchovies dissolve. Add the spinach, drained currants, and pine nuts. Add a good grating of nutmeg, taste, season with salt and pepper to taste, and stir-fry for about 5 minutes until heated through, glossy, and well mixed. Serve immediately.

pasta, bread, and pizza

8 small potatoes, halved

12 oz. linguine or tagliatelle

5 oz. fine green beans

sea salt

PESTO ALLA GENOVESE

½ cup pine nuts,
lightly toasted in a skillet

3 garlic cloves, crushed
then chopped

¾ cup torn fresh basil leaves

½ teaspoon coarse sea salt

⅓ cup freshly grated
Parmesan cheese

⅓ cup freshly grated
pecorino cheese

⅓ cup extra virgin olive oil

SERVES 4

Real Italian pesto is an exuberantly intense, rich paste of garlic, basil, and cheese, given extra texture with pine nuts. Ligurians take pride in this culinary masterpiece: they say that the basil in their part of the Mediterranean has particular pungency. Aficionados suggest that half Parmesan and half pecorino cheeses will make the best pesto; others use only one type; some even add ricotta. Don't make the pesto too smooth: it should retain some texture and bite.

linguine with pesto alla genovese

To make the pesto, grind the pine nuts, garlic, basil, and salt to a paste with a mortar and pestle or in a food processor, using the pulse button.

Keep stirring the paste with one hand (or have the machine still running) while you gradually add half the cheese, then half the olive oil. Repeat the process until you have a rich, stiff, vividly green paste or sauce.

Bring a large saucepan of water to a boil, then add a large pinch of salt. Add the potatoes and cook for 5 minutes. Add the pasta and cook until al dente, about 8 minutes more. After about 4 minutes, add the green beans. Drain and transfer to a large serving bowl. Add the pesto, toss well, and serve immediately.

Note Fresh pesto is best used within hours, although it will keep for up to 1 week in the refrigerator if sealed in an airtight container.

sicilian spaghetti

Olive oil, garlic, and assertive Mediterranean vegetables combine to produce this substantial pasta dish. The tiny tomato halves are oven-roasted and the cubes of eggplant salted, then sautéed, to intensify the tastes. The sauce is relatively dry and minimal and the dish is topped with handfuls of basil. Use whatever sturdy dry pasta is available: spaghetti, penne, and rigatoni all taste excellent with this sauce.

Bring a large saucepan of salted water to a boil, ready to add the pasta when the vegetables are half cooked.

Put the eggplant cubes in a nonmetal bowl, then add 1 teaspoon salt and set aside while you cook the tomatoes.

Pack the tomatoes, cut sides up, on an oven tray, sprinkle with the remaining salt, and drizzle with 2 tablespoons of the olive oil. Roast in a preheated oven at 450°F for 10 minutes or until wilted and aromatic.

Cook the pasta until al dente or according to the package instructions.

Drain the eggplant and pat dry with paper towels. Heat 4 tablespoons of the olive oil in a nonstick skillet. Add the eggplant and cook, stirring, over high heat until frizzled and soft, about 8 minutes. Add the roasted tomato halves, tomato juice, garlic, and black pepper. Cook, stirring, for 2–3 minutes, then tear up most of the basil leaves and stir through. Test the pasta to make sure it is cooked, then drain.

Return the pasta to the saucepan and toss in the remaining olive oil. Divide between heated bowls, spoon over the sauce, add a few fresh basil leaves, and serve.

1 eggplant, about 12 oz., cut into ½-inch cubes

1 lb. cherry tomatoes, halved and seeded

½ cup extra virgin olive oil

14 oz. pasta, such as spaghetti or penne

½ cup tomato juice

2 garlic cloves, chopped

sea salt and freshly ground black pepper

leaves from a large bunch of fresh basil, to serve

SERVES 4

Resplendent with elegant ingredients such as lobster, shrimp, or crab, this pasta dish is a real treat for a special occasion. You can buy the lobster meat ready-prepared from a fish seller and it is deceptively easy to put together.

pappardelle with seafood sauce

Bring a large saucepan of salted water to a boil, ready to add the pasta once you have made the seafood sauce.

To make the sauce, heat the olive oil in a heavy skillet. Add the lobster, shrimp, or crabmeat, dill, chives, and 1 tablespoon of the lemon juice, then season with salt and pepper. Heat briefly until the flavors blend well. Leave on a very low heat to keep warm.

Cook the pasta until al dente or according to the package instructions. Drain, then tip into the seafood sauce. Toss gently with 2 wooden spoons, add the lemon peel, and divide between 4 pasta bowls.

12 oz. pappardelle or tagliatelle

SEAFOOD SAUCE

¾ cup extra virgin olive oil

1 lb. lobster meat, from
2 lb. whole lobster, or shrimp
or crabmeat

a bunch of fresh dill, chopped,
about 1 cup

a bunch of fresh chives,
chopped, about 1 cup

grated peel and freshly
squeezed juice of 1 lemon

sea salt and freshly ground
black pepper

SERVES 4

The clams are the stars of this dish, but it's crucial that the sauce is smooth. If you only have canned tomatoes, purée them with a hand blender or press them through a strainer before using. Delicious as this is, it's not an elegant meal to eat, so be prepared: tie your napkin firmly round your neck and use your fingers to pick the clams from their shells.

pasta con le vongole

2 tablespoons olive oil

2 garlic cloves, finely chopped

a sprig of fresh rosemary

2¼ cups canned
crushed tomatoes

½ teaspoon sugar

10 oz. dried pasta, such as
spaghetti or linguine

2¼ lb. fresh baby clams in shells

2 tablespoons chopped,
fresh flatleaf parsley

sea salt and freshly
ground black pepper

SERVES 4

Heat the olive oil in a saucepan, add the garlic and rosemary, and cook for 2 minutes. Add the crushed tomatoes and sugar, then season with salt and pepper to taste. Bring to a boil, cover, and simmer for 30 minutes, then remove and discard the sprig of rosemary.

Meanwhile, bring a large saucepan of water to a boil. Add a pinch of salt, then add the pasta, and cook until al dente, or according to the package instructions.

While the pasta is cooking, put the clams and 2 tablespoons water into another large saucepan. Cover and cook over medium heat for 4–5 minutes, shaking the pan occasionally until all the shells have opened, and discarding any that remain closed.

Strain the clam cooking juices through a sieve into the tomato pan, to remove grit. When the clams are cool enough to handle, shell half of them and discard the empty shells. Add the shelled and unshelled clams to the tomato sauce and simmer for 3–4 minutes.

Drain the pasta and return it to the warm pan. Add the clams and parsley and toss to mix. Divide between 4 bowls and serve.

A classic, this famous dish was named, some say, after the charcoal burners or coalmen (carbonari) from Umbria and Lazio in Italy. Others believe it may have come about during World War II, with American soldiers bringing their wartime rations of bacon and eggs. Whatever the origins, it is delicious and very quick to make. The cheese, though optional, is frequently included, as is the cream.

spaghetti alla carbonara

Bring a large saucepan of water to a boil, then add a large pinch of salt. Add the spaghetti and cook until al dente or according to the package instructions.

Put the prosciutto in a heavy skillet and cook until the fat runs and the prosciutto is cooked but barely crisp. Add the garlic and remove from the heat.

Put the eggs, salt, and pepper in a bowl and beat well, adding the cream, if using. Set aside.

As soon as the spaghetti is ready, drain it and put the skillet back over high heat. Toss in the hot pasta, then stir in the eggs and half of the Parmesan, if using, to make a creamy sauce. Remove from the heat. Toss, using tongs, to mix everything well. Serve with the remaining Parmesan, if using, on top.

14 oz. spaghetti

6 oz. prosciutto or thinly sliced bacon, cut into 1-inch pieces

2 garlic cloves, crushed then chopped

3 large eggs

2 tablespoons thick cream (optional)

1 cup freshly grated Parmesan cheese (optional)

sea salt and freshly ground black pepper

SERVES 4

Focaccia literally means "a bread that was baked on the hearth," but it is easy to bake in conventional ovens. It is found in many different forms, and can be thin and crisp, thick and soft, round or square. Serve with olive oil, some balsamic vinegar for dipping, and a handful of olives.

rosemary focaccia

5 cups Italian-style flour, or all-purpose flour, plus extra for kneading

½ teaspoon fine sea salt

1½ cakes compressed fresh yeast or 1 envelope active dry yeast, ¼ oz.

⅔ cup extra virgin olive oil

2 cups hand-hot water

coarse sea or crystal salt

sprigs of rosemary

a water spray

2 shallow cake pans, pie or pizza plates, 10 inches in diameter, lightly oiled

MAKES 2 LOAVES

Sift the flour and salt into a large bowl and make a hollow in the center. Crumble in the fresh yeast. For dried yeast, follow the package instructions. Pour in 3 tablespoons of the olive oil, then rub in the yeast until the mixture resembles fine bread crumbs. Pour in the hot water and mix with your hands until the dough comes together.

Transfer the dough to a floured surface, wash and dry your hands, and knead for 10 minutes until smooth and elastic. The dough should be quite soft, but if too soft to handle, knead in more flour, 1 tablespoon at a time. Put the dough in a clean, oiled bowl, cover with a damp tea towel or plastic wrap and let rise in a warm place until doubled in size, about 30 minutes–1½ hours.

Punch down the dough and cut in half. Put on a floured surface and shape each half into a round ball. Roll out into 2 circles, 10 inches in diameter, and put in the tins. Cover with a damp dish towel or plastic wrap and let rise for 30 minutes.

Remove the dish towel and, using your finger tips, make dimples all over the surface of the dough. They can be quite deep. Pour over the remaining oil and sprinkle generously with coarse salt. Cover again and let rise for 30 minutes. Spray with water, sprinkle the rosemary on top and bake in a preheated oven at 400°F for 20–25 minutes. Transfer to a wire rack to cool. Eat the same day or freeze immediately.

Fougasse belongs to the same ancient family of breads as focaccie, the original hearth breads (page 191). In Provence, these flat, slashed "ladder breads" (so called because of their shapes) are highly decorative and often flavored with olives or herbs. Sweeter versions contain orange-flower water and almonds and are associated with feast days.

fougasse

Put the olive oil, water, and honey in a measuring jug and stir to dissolve. Put the flour, yeast, and salt in a food processor. With the motor running, pour the liquid through the feed tube to form a dense dough. Stop, then repeat for 30 seconds more, to develop the gluten.

Transfer the dough to a large, oiled bowl, and cover with an oiled plastic bag. Leave in a warm place for at least 30 minutes or up to 2 hours until doubled in volume.

Punch down the risen dough, transfer to a well-floured work surface and knead for 5–8 minutes or until silky and smooth. Return to the bowl, cover, and let rise again for 20 minutes or until doubled in size, then divide into 2. Squeeze, pat, and knead each ball into an oval. Pat or roll out each oval on an oiled baking sheet, until it

is 3 times its original size, and about ½ inch thick. Repeat the process with the second fougasse.

Make 2 rows of diagonal slashes in the dough, then open up the slashes to make larger holes. Tug out at the ends and sides if you'd like to open up the dough even more.

Brush the two breads all over with olive oil, then sprinkle with warm water. Add your choice of garlic, onion, olives, orange peel, or orange-flower water.

Bake each fougasse towards the top of a preheated oven at 425°F for 15–20 minutes or until risen, crusty, but still chewy. Repeat with the other 2 portions of dough.

Serve warm and eat with your fingers, pulling the bread into short lengths.

¼ cup extra virgin olive oil, plus extra for baking

2 cups lukewarm water

2 teaspoons honey or syrup (optional)

1⅔ cups whole-wheat flour (or 1⅓ cups malted whole-wheat flour plus ⅓ cup buckwheat, triticale, or spelt flour)

3½ cups bread flour, plus extra for kneading

1 envelope active dry yeast, ¼ oz.

2 teaspoons sea salt

warm water, for baking

TOPPINGS

your choice of:

sliced garlic

onion rings

black olives, cut into strips

orange peel, thinly sliced

orange-flower water

2 large baking sheets, oiled

MAKES 4 LOAVES

pissaladière

Packed with the flavors of Provence in southern France, this pizza-like bread is ideal picnic food. Soft, sweet onions scented with Provençal herbs are spread over a layer of tomato sauce, then topped with red bell pepper strips or sea-salty anchovies and black olives, all on a thin base.

3 tablespoons olive oil

3 lb. mild onions, thinly sliced

3 garlic cloves, chopped

1 teaspoon dried herbes de Provence

TOMATO SAUCE

2 tablespoons olive oil

4 cups canned chopped tomatoes

3 tablespoons tomato paste

1 tablespoon capers, rinsed and drained

⅔ cup dry white wine

sea salt and freshly ground black pepper

YEAST DOUGH

1 cake compressed fresh yeast or 1 teaspoon dry active yeast

a pinch of sugar

1 cup all-purpose flour, plus extra for rolling

4 tablespoons unsalted butter, chilled and chopped

1 egg, beaten

a pinch of sea salt

TO FINISH

red bell pepper strips or about 10 anchovy fillets (optional)

olive oil, for drizzling

12–18 small black olives

a jelly-roll pan, 13 x 8 inches

SERVES 4–6

Heat the olive oil in a large saucepan, add the onions and garlic, and stir well to coat with the oil. Add 1–2 tablespoons water, cover tightly, and simmer over very low heat for about 1 hour until meltingly soft. Stir the onions from time to time to prevent them sticking, but don't let them color. Add a little more water if they look dry. Stir in the herbs. Drain the mixture into a strainer over a bowl and reserve the liquid for the yeast dough.

To make the tomato sauce, heat the olive oil in a saucepan, add the tomatoes, tomato paste, capers, white wine, salt, and pepper. Mix well and bring to a boil. Simmer, uncovered, for about 1 hour, stirring occasionally, until well reduced and very thick. Taste and adjust the seasoning. Set aside.

To make the yeast dough, cream the fresh yeast in a bowl with the sugar, then beat in 3 tablespoons of the warmed reserved onion liquid. Leave for 10 minutes until frothy. For dry yeast, follow the package instructions. Sift the flour into a bowl and rub in the butter. Make a hollow in the center, add the egg, yeast mixture, and a pinch of salt, and mix to a very soft dough—add more onion liquid if it seems dry. Knead in the bowl for 1–2 minutes until smooth. Put in an oiled bowl, cover with plastic wrap, and let rise for 1 hour or until doubled in size.

Punch down the dough, knead lightly, then roll out on a lightly floured surface. Use to line the jelly-roll pan, pushing the dough well up the edges. Spread the reduced tomato sauce thinly over the dough base. Cover with the onions. Arrange the red bell pepper strips, if using, in a lattice on top of the onions. Alternatively, cut the anchovy fillets in half lengthwise and use them instead. Drizzle with a little olive oil and bake in a preheated oven at 375°F for about 1 hour until the pastry is golden and crisp. Arrange the olives on top and serve warm or cold.

Something like a double-thickness, well-stuffed pizza, this ancient recipe is really a kind of substantial double-crust pie. Vary ingredients as you like, though these are fairly typical for a Sicilian recipe—food from this island is often packed with intense flavors.

sicilian schiacciata

Put the flour, sugar, salt, and yeast into a food processor. Pulse a few times to mix and sift.

Put the warm water, egg and olive oil in a bowl or jug and whisk well. With the machine running, add the mixture to the processor through the feed tube. The dough will form, clump, then gather in a mass. Remove to a well-floured work surface, sprinkle with extra flour, and knead the dough for 2–3 minutes or until smooth and silky.

Put the ball of dough into a lightly oiled bowl and enclose in a large plastic bag. Leave in a warm place until doubled in size, about 1 hour. Remove from the bowl and punch down the dough. Cut it in half, then roll, pat, and stretch each piece to about 12 inches in diameter.

Stretch one of the rounds to about 1 inch more and slide onto a heavy baking tray. Sprinkle it with the cheese, the anchovies and their oil, the prosciutto, onions, tomatoes, olives, and chili. Wet your fingers and sprinkle some drops of water all over and around the edges.

Press the remaining round of dough on top. Push down with your knuckles to seal, then use a fork to press and prick all over in a decorative pattern. Press your fingertips all over to make deep indentations. Wet both hands and sprinkle more water on top, then sprinkle with the olive oil, salt, pepper, and oregano. Let rise in a warm place for about 1 hour or almost doubled in size.

Bake in a preheated oven at 475°F for 15 minutes, then reduce the heat to 400°F and cook for a further 25–30 minutes or until crisp, golden, and fragrant— it should sound hollow when you tap the bottom of the loaf with your knuckles.

Eat hot or warm in squares, segments, or pulled into chunks.

3⅓ cups bread flour, plus extra for shaping

2 tablespoons sugar

1½ teaspoons salt

1 envelope active dry yeast, ¼ oz.

1¼ cups lukewarm water

1 large egg, beaten

2 tablespoons extra virgin olive oil

FILLING

6 oz. caciocavallo or scamorza cheese (smoked mozzarella), chopped or sliced

2 oz. canned anchovies with their oil

4 slices (about 3 oz.) prosciutto or other cured Italian ham, pulled into pieces

2 red or white onions, sliced finely into rings, blanched in boiling water and drained

8 sun-dried tomatoes in oil, chopped

16 green or black olives, pitted

1–1½ teaspoons crumbled dried red chili

1 tablespoon extra virgin olive oil

1 teaspoon sea salt

2 teaspoons cracked black peppercorns

1 teaspoon dried oregano or 2 teaspoons fresh, chopped oregano

SERVES 4–6

1⅔ cups fine Italian semolina flour (farina di semola)

½ cup compressed fresh yeast or 1 teaspoon active dry yeast

1 tablespoon freshly squeezed lemon juice

1 tablespoon olive oil

a pinch of sea salt

about 1¼ cups warm water

SALSA PIZZAIOLA

½ cup olive oil

2 garlic cloves, chopped

1 teaspoon dried oregano

1¾ lb. fresh tomatoes, peeled and coarsely chopped, or canned chopped tomatoes

sea salt and freshly ground black pepper

PIZZA TOPPING

8 oz. fresh mozzarella cheese, thinly sliced

a large handful of fresh basil leaves

olive oil, for drizzling

sea salt and freshly ground black pepper

a "testa" or terra cotta bakestone or 2 large, heavy baking sheets

MAKES 2 PIZZAS

This classic pizza was originally made in honor of Queen Margherita of Naples, symbolizing the Italian national flag, with its green, white, and red topping.

pizza alla margherita

Put the bakestone or baking sheets in the oven and preheat to 425°F.

To make the dough, put the semolina flour in a bowl and crumble the fresh yeast into the flour. For dry yeast, follow the package instructions. Add the lemon juice, olive oil, and a generous pinch of salt, then add enough warm water to form a very soft dough. Transfer to a floured surface and knead for 10 minutes or until smooth and elastic. Put the dough in a clean, oiled bowl (or an oiled plastic bag), cover, and let rise until doubled in size (about 1 hour).

Meanwhile, make the salsa pizzaiola. Put the olive oil in a large shallow pan and heat almost to smoking point. Standing back (it will splutter if it's at the right temperature), add the garlic, oregano, and tomatoes. Cook over a fierce heat for 5–8 minutes or until thick and glossy. Season with salt and pepper.

Cut the dough in half and knead each half into a round. Pat or roll the rounds into 10-inch circles, keeping the bases well floured. Transfer the pizzas onto baking sheets lined with nonstick parchment paper. Spread each one lightly with salsa pizzaiola, cover with sliced mozzarella, and season with salt and pepper. Let rise in a warm place for 10 minutes, then open the oven door, and slide paper and pizza onto the hot bakestone or baking sheets. If you are brave, try to shoot them into the oven so that they leave the paper behind—this takes practice.

Bake for 18–20 minutes, until the crust is golden and the cheese melted but still white. Remove from the oven, sprinkle with basil leaves, and drizzle with olive oil, then eat immediately.

1 cake compressed fresh yeast, 1 tablespoon active dry yeast

a pinch of sugar

1 cup lukewarm water

2½ cups all-purpose flour, plus extra for dusting

1 tablespoon olive oil, plus extra for brushing

a pinch of salt

FILLING

4 oz. cubed melting cheese, such as mozzarella

3 oz. cubed salami, ham, or cooked sausage

⅓ cup cooked, chopped spinach

4 sun-dried tomatoes in oil, chopped

3–4 tablespoons Salsa Pizzaiola (page 198)

2–3 tablespoons chopped mixed herbs

sea salt and freshly ground black pepper

SERVES 2

Italians are thrifty, and a really delicious double-crust pizza can be made with a carefully chosen mixture of leftovers. There must be cheese to keep it moist, but you can add anchovies, cooked meat sauce, capers, or olives—whatever you like, as long as their flavors suit each other.

pizza rustica

To make the dough, put the fresh yeast and sugar in a medium bowl and beat until creamy. Beat in the warm water and leave for 10 minutes until frothy. For dry yeast, follow the package instructions.

Sift the flour into a large bowl and make a hollow in the center. Pour in the yeast mixture, olive oil, and a large pinch of salt. Mix with a round-bladed knife, then your hands, until the dough comes together. Transfer to a floured surface, wash and dry your hands, and knead for 10 minutes until smooth and elastic. The dough should be quite soft, but if too soft to handle, add more flour, 1 tablespoon at a time. Put the dough in a clean, oiled bowl, cover with a damp dish towel or plastic wrap, and let rise until doubled in size—about 1 hour.

To make the filling, put the mozzarella, salami, spinach, sun-dried tomatoes, salsa pizzaiola, and mixed herbs in a bowl and season with salt and pepper.

Roll out the dough to a large circle, making sure it is well floured so it doesn't stick. Pile the filling onto one half of the dough, avoiding the edges. Flip over the other half to cover, press the edges together to seal, then twist and crimp. Slide onto a floured baking sheet and brush lightly with olive oil. Make a slash in the top to prevent it exploding when cooking.

Bake in a preheated oven at 425°F for about 25 minutes until golden and firm. Remove from the oven, set aside for 5 minutes, then serve.

turkish pizza turnover

3 cups bread flour, plus extra
for kneading

1½ teaspoons active dry yeast

1½ teaspoons sea salt

1 tablespoon extra virgin
olive oil

½–⅔ cup lukewarm water

CHEESE AND SPINACH FILLING

1 lb. spinach leaves

1 tablespoon extra virgin
olive oil

1 small onion, finely chopped

2 garlic cloves, crushed

4 oz. feta cheese, crumbled

2 tablespoons grated
Parmesan cheese

2 tablespoons
mascarpone cheese

a little freshly grated nutmeg

freshly ground black pepper

a flat griddle or large heavy skillet

SERVES 4

These turnovers are similar to the Italian "calzone" or stuffed pizza. They are sold in Turkish markets, cut into thin strips. They can also be cooked on a barbecue with a flat plate—brush the bread with olive oil and cook for 5 minutes, turning once.

Sift the flour into the bowl of an electric mixer* with dough hook attached. Stir in the yeast and salt. Add the olive oil and warm water and work until the dough is smooth and elastic.

Meanwhile, to make the filling, discard any thick spinach stalks, then wash the leaves in a colander. Drain, transfer to a large saucepan, and heat gently for 2–3 minutes until the leaves have wilted. Rinse under cold water, drain completely, and squeeze out as much water as possible. Finely chop the spinach and set aside.

Heat the olive oil in a skillet, add the onion and garlic, and fry gently for 5 minutes until very soft and lightly golden. Stir in the spinach, cheeses, nutmeg, and pepper, then remove from the heat.

Transfer the dough back onto a floured surface and knead it gently. Divide the dough into 4 equal pieces and roll out each piece to a rectangle 8 x 16 inches (it will be very thin). Spread a quarter of the spinach mixture over half the dough, fold over, and seal the edges. Repeat with the other pieces of dough to make 4 turnovers.

Cook on a flat griddle or large, heavy skillet. Serve hot.

*Note If you don't have an electric mixer, use a food processor with the plastic blade attachment, or make by hand in a large mixing bowl. Gradually work the mixture together with your hands to form a soft dough, then turn out onto a lightly floured surface and knead for 8–10 minutes until the dough becomes smooth and elastic.

sweet things and drinks

⅔ cup light cream and milk, mixed half and half

peel of 1 lemon, cut into 8 long strips, bruised

¼ cup sugar

3 large eggs

2 teaspoons pure vanilla extract

¼ cup sugar, to glaze

4 shallow heatproof dishes, ½ cup each

a baking pan

a cook's blowtorch (optional)

SERVES 4

These superb caramelized egg custards scented with strips of lemon peel are one of the joys of Spain. This version is from Catalonia. Often they are made in small, shallow, individual earthenware dishes, called cazuelas (page 33). Catalonia once briefly included Sicily, Sardinia, and Naples, so there are interesting culinary influences from these neighboring cuisines. You can caramelize the sugar under a hot broiler or use a blowtorch if you have one. Be sure to have the heat source very hot—you do not want to damage, melt, or toughen the delicate custard beneath by undue browning.

spanish flans

Put the cream and milk, and 4 of the strips of lemon peel in a saucepan and heat almost to boiling (this is called scalding). Put the pan in a bowl of ice water to cool it quickly. Put the sugar, eggs, and vanilla in a bowl and whisk until well blended, trying to avoid making froth. Stir in the cooled scalded cream.

Pour the custard mixture into the 4 dishes, then tuck one of the remaining strips of lemon peel into each custard.

Set the dishes in a baking pan and add enough boiling water to come halfway up the sides of the dishes. Bake toward the top of a preheated oven at 300°F for 20 minutes or until very gently set and wobbly. Remove the baking pan from the oven, then remove the dishes from the pan.

To glaze the custards, sprinkle the sugar evenly over each one. Preheat an overhead broiler to very hot, leaving space for the pots to be 1 inch from the heat. Alternatively, turn on a blowtorch. Broil or blowtorch the custards until a fine layer of caramel forms on top. Serve, preferably at room temperature, within 2 hours.

*The secret of a great panna cotta
is in the wobble. Panna cotta means
"cooked or scalded cream" and is
said to have originated in Piedmont
or Lombardy, where the cream and
milk are very rich.*

2 cups heavy cream

1¼ cups whole milk

1 vanilla bean, split

¼ cup superfine sugar

3 teaspoons powdered gelatin

CANDIED ORANGE PEEL

2 oranges

¼ cup sugar

6 molds, about ½ cup each

SERVES 6

panna cotta with candied orange peel

To make the panna cotta, put the cream and milk, split vanilla bean, and sugar in a saucepan and bring to a boil. Sprinkle the gelatin into the cream and stir until dissolved. Cool, then chill in the refrigerator until it just begins to thicken. At this stage, stir the cream briskly to distribute the vanilla seeds, then remove the vanilla bean. (Rinse and dry and keep in the sugar jar.) Pour into the molds, set on a tray, and refrigerate for at least 5 hours or until set.

Remove the peel from the oranges with a sharp potato peeler (removing any bitter white pith with a knife afterward). Cut the peel into long, fine shreds. Bring a small saucepan of water to a boil and blanch the shreds for 1 minute. Drain, then refresh in cold water.

Put the sugar and ½ cup water in a small saucepan and stir until dissolved. Add the orange shreds and bring to a rolling boil. Boil for 2–3 minutes, then strain the shreds and transfer to a plate to cool. Before they cool too much, separate them out so they don't stick together.

To serve, press the top of the panna cotta and gently pull away from the edge of the mold (this breaks the airlock). Carefully invert onto a small cold plate. (Give the mold a good shake and the panna cotta should drop out.) If it still won't turn out, dip very briefly into warm water, then invert onto the plate and lift off. Top with the orange shreds and a spoonful of syrup.

Strawberries, when freshly picked and at the height of their summery sweetness, are a joy: they should be simply eaten on their own. At other times strawberries may need a little assistance to coax out their full potential, as in this recipe.

sugared strawberries

To make the spiced sugar, put the cinnamon, peppercorns, sugar, and lemon peel in an electric coffee grinder or small spice grinder. Grind in continuous bursts to make a powdery spiced mixture.

Put the strawberries in a bowl and spoon half the mixture on top, gently stirring and mixing to encourage the juices to run. Leave for 10 minutes. Meanwhile, press the ricotta through a sieve into a bowl with the back of a spoon. Mix in the liqueur, the remaining spiced sugar, and the vinegar to form a cream.

To serve, put spoonfuls of the creamy mixture in small, stemmed glasses or glass or china dishes, then pile the berries on top, and sprinkle them with a few extra drops of liqueur.

2 pints ripe, red strawberries, washed, dried, hulled, and halved

8 oz. fresh ricotta cheese

1 tablespoon Amaretto liqueur, plus extra to serve

½ teaspoon balsamic vinegar

SPICED SUGAR

½ stick of cinnamon, crushed

6 peppercorns, crushed

⅓ cup sugar

3-inch strip of lemon peel

SERVES 4

This ice cream really does taste like an Italian gelato. It is silky smooth and heavenly, served in a glass coppa with delicious warmed Amarena cherries. Amarena cherries are sold in pretty white and blue glass jars—a great souvenir of a vacation in Italy, but they are less expensive bought in cans from an Italian gourmet store.

vanilla gelato with hot cherry sauce

1 vanilla bean, split

5 cups whole milk

2 tablespoons non-fat dry milk

¼ cup cornstarch

1⅓ cups sugar

1 teaspoon pure vanilla extract

13 oz. canned Italian Amarena cherries in syrup

2 tablespoons maraschino or kirsch

an ice cream maker (optional)

SERVES 6

Put the split vanilla bean in a saucepan with 4 cups of the milk, then beat in the dry milk. Bring to boiling point, turn off the heat, and leave to infuse for 20 minutes.

Remove the vanilla bean and scrape out the seeds into the milk. Beat the seeds through the milk. Wash and dry the bean and store in the sugar jar.

Dissolve the cornstarch in the remaining milk, then pour into the hot milk, and add the sugar. Set over the heat again and bring to a boil, stirring constantly until thickened. Cover the surface with plastic wrap and let cool to room temperature. Stir in the vanilla extract. Chill, then churn in an ice cream maker for 20–25 minutes or until set.

Alternatively, pour into a shallow freezer tray and freeze until frozen around the edges. Mash well with a fork. When it is half-frozen again, blend in a food processor until creamy, then cover and freeze until firm. Let soften in the refrigerator for 20 minutes before serving.

When ready to serve, put the cherries, their syrup, and the liqueur in a saucepan and heat gently. Serve the ice cream in large scoops with the sauce trickled over it.

bitter chocolate and hazelnut gelato

½ cup blanched hazelnuts, finely chopped

1 cup vanilla sugar or superfine sugar

⅔ cup whole milk

8 oz. bittersweet chocolate, broken in pieces

1 tablespoon corn syrup

1 tablespoon chocolate or hazelnut liqueur or dark rum

1¾ cups heavy cream

crisp wafers or cookies, to serve (optional)

an electric ice cream maker or a 1-quart freezerproof container

SERVES 4–6

Italian and French gelaterias offer splendid, often simple flavor combinations when it comes to ice cream. Chocolate and nuts are particularly delicious, especially if the chocolate is of the high-quality, bittersweet type. If you have a pestle and mortar, try to pound the nuts and sugar to a very smooth texture—otherwise use an electric coffee grinder or spice grinder in short bursts.

Put the chopped hazelnuts in a dry skillet and dry-cook over medium heat, stirring constantly until they darken and smell toasty, about 2–3 minutes (take care, because they burn easily). Pour out onto a plate and let cool.

Put the toasted hazelnuts and ¼ cup of the sugar in a small electric spice grinder or coffee grinder. Grind in brief bursts, to a smooth, speckly powder.

Put the milk, chocolate, and remaining sugar in a saucepan over very gentle heat. Cook until the chocolate melts, stirring constantly, then add the corn syrup and ground sugar and nuts. Remove from the heat, put the pan into a bowl of ice water and let cool. Stir in the liqueur and cream and cool again.

Pour the prepared mixture into the ice cream maker and churn for 20–25 minutes or until set. Alternatively, freeze in the container, covered, for 6 hours, beating and whisking it once, after 3 hours.

Serve in scoops with wafers or cookies, if using.

A beautiful, pink, exotic sorbetto from Sicily, delicately perfumed with a hint of cinnamon or jasmine flower water. Just for fun, the chocolate chips represent the black watermelon seeds, but they do add a nice crunchy texture. You won't need a whole watermelon for this recipe, so keep the rest to eat on its own or make into a fruit salad.

watermelon sorbet with chocolate chip seeds

1½ lb. red watermelon flesh, cut into cubes

¾ cup sugar (or a bit less if the melon is very sweet)

1 small cinnamon stick

freshly squeezed juice of 2 ripe lemons

a little pink food color, if necessary

⅓ cup semisweet chocolate chips

an ice cream maker or a shallow freezer tray, 1 inch deep

SERVES 4–6

Remove the seeds from the melon with the tip of a small knife. Put the flesh in a food processor and purée until smooth. With the machine running, pour in the sugar and blend for 30 seconds.

Pour the melon mixture into a saucepan and add the cinnamon stick. Slowly bring to a boil, stirring all the time to dissolve the sugar completely, then turn down the heat to a bare simmer for 1 minute. Remove from the heat, add the lemon juice, and a few drops of pink food color if necessary.

Let cool. When cold, remove the cinnamon stick and chill the mixture in the refrigerator for at least 1 hour (or overnight—this makes freezing quicker).

Transfer to an ice cream maker and freeze according to the manufacturer's instructions. Stir in the chocolate chips when the sorbetto is still soft. Transfer to a chilled freezer container, cover, and freeze until firm. Let soften in the refrigerator for 20 minutes before serving.

Alternatively, pour into a shallow freezer tray and freeze until the sorbetto is frozen around the edges. Mash well with a fork. When it is half frozen again, blend in a food processor until creamy, stir in the chocolate chips, then cover and freeze until firm. Let soften in the refrigerator for 20 minutes before serving.

This Sicilian granita is superbly refreshing. The blanched almonds are blended with sugar and ice water to form a sweet milk-like liquid and the Amaretto liqueur adds extra almond flavor.

almond milk granita, laced with amaretto

Put the almonds and sugar in a food processor and grind as finely as you can. Add 2 cups of the ice water and process for 2–3 minutes until very milky.

Pour this mixture into the blender with the remaining 2 cups ice water (you may have to do this in 2 batches). Blend on high speed for 2–3 minutes to grind the almonds as finely as possible. Pour into a bowl or pitcher, cover, and transfer to the refrigerator for several hours or overnight for the almonds to settle. Strain the settled almond milk from the sediment through a fine strainer or cheesecloth into the freezer tray. Stir in the Amaretto.

Cover and freeze for about 30 minutes, until the edges start to freeze. Scrape the frozen edges into the center with a fork and mash the mixture evenly. Repeat every 30 minutes until it forms a mound of shimmering ice crystals. Serve in chilled glasses with your prettiest silver spoons.

⅔ **cup blanched almonds**

½ **cup sugar**

1 **quart ice water**

3 **tablespoons Amaretto liqueur**

a shallow freezer tray,
1 inch deep

SERVES 8

Lemon tart—wobbly, sharp, creamy, but acidic—is an outrageously delicious dish. In France, a tarte au citron is often a slim, very elegant offering, not heavily filled. The ideal is to make it a few hours before you intend to eat it, then serve it warm or cool. Some ice-cold scoops of thick, sharp heavy cream are the perfect accompaniment. Serve with a small glass of citrus liqueur, dark rum, or brandy.

classic lemon tart

6 tablespoons confectioners' sugar, sifted

1½ sticks butter, at room temperature

2 large egg yolks

2 tablespoons ice water

1⅔ cups all-purpose flour, sifted

LEMON FILLING

4 large eggs

¾ cup sugar

2 tablespoons grated lemon peel from 2–3 lemons

½ cup heavy cream, plus extra to serve

a round springform tart pan, 8 inches in diameter and 1 inch deep, set on a baking sheet

parchment paper and baking beans

SERVES 4

To make the dough, set aside 2 tablespoons of the confectioners' sugar and put the remainder in the bowl of an electric mixer. Add the butter and beat until creamy, soft, and white. Add the egg yolks one at a time and continue beating until well mixed. Trickle in half the ice water, then add the flour. Beat on a lower speed, adding the remaining water until the dough gathers into a soft ball. Wrap in plastic wrap and chill for 40–60 minutes.

Transfer the dough to a floured work surface and roll out to ¼ inch thick. Use it to line the tart pan. Gently push the dough into the corners. Cut off the excess dough. Chill for a further 20 minutes or until very firm.

Prick the dough all over with a fork, line with parchment paper, fill with baking beans, and bake blind in a preheated oven at 350°F for 15 minutes. Remove the paper and the beans. Let the pastry rest for 5 minutes, then bake again for 10 minutes or until pale golden.

To make the filling, put the eggs, sugar, and half the lemon peel in a bowl and beat well for 2 minutes with a electric beater. Stir in the lemon juice and heavy cream, then pour the mixture into the pastry case. Bake at 250°F for 35 minutes, or until the filling is barely set.

While the tart cooks, put the remaining lemon peel in a strainer, pour over boiling water, then refresh under cold running water. Put the peel, the reserved 2 tablespoons confectioners' sugar, and 4 tablespoons water in a saucepan over low heat. Cook gently until the peel looks syrupy. Sprinkle the peel over the cooked tart. Serve hot or warm, with additional spoonfuls of heavy cream.

You'll find simple tarts made with seasonal fruit all over Italy. The ricotta makes a lovely light cheesecake with a slightly grainy texture. Be sure to try this only with fresh figs—dried are not the same. If figs aren't in season, all sorts of other fruits can be used to top the tart.

caramelized fig tart

6 tablespoons butter, softened

6 tablespoons sugar

3 egg yolks

½ teaspoon pure vanilla extract

1 generous cup all-purpose flour, plus extra for dusting

1 teaspoon salt

1 egg yolk, beaten, for brushing

FIG FILLING

8 oz. fresh ricotta cheese

1 stick plus 1 tablespoon butter, softened

⅔ cup sugar or vanilla sugar

2 eggs

8–10 ripe black figs (depending on size), cut in halves or quarters

raspberry jelly

a round springform tart pan, 8 inches in diameter

baking beans

SERVES 6

To make the dough, put the butter, sugar, the 3 egg yolks, and vanilla extract in a food processor and blend until smooth.

Sift the flour and salt onto a sheet of parchment paper. Shoot the flour into the food processor and blend until just mixed.

Transfer to a floured work surface and knead gently until smooth. Form into a ball, flatten, and wrap in plastic wrap. Chill for at least 30 minutes.

To make the filling, put the ricotta, butter, and sugar in a bowl and beat until smooth. Put the 2 eggs in another bowl, beat well, then gradually beat them into the cheese mixture. Set aside.

Roll out the dough thinly and use to line the tart pan. Prick the base all over with a fork, then chill or freeze for 15 minutes. Line with aluminum foil and baking beans, set on a baking sheet, and bake blind in the center of a preheated oven at 375°F for 10–12 minutes. Remove the foil and beans, brush with the beaten egg yolk, and cook for a further 5 minutes until golden.

Remove the pie crust from the oven, let it cool slightly, then pour the filling into it, and bake for a further 25–30 minutes until risen and brown.

Remove from the oven and let cool in the pan for 10 minutes, then transfer to a wire rack to cool completely. Arrange the figs, cut side up, on top of the tart. Warm the raspberry jelly and lightly brush the figs with it.

Protect the edges of the pie crust with foil to prevent over-browning. Preheat the broiler and set the tart close to the heat. Broil quickly until the figs are just browning, then serve immediately.

greek honey, walnut, and brandy cake

½ cup extra virgin olive oil

½ cup sugar

2 eggs

2 cups walnut pieces

1½ cups self-rising flour, sieved

¼ teaspoon salt

½ cup strained plain yogurt or thick-set yogurt

2 tablespoons brandy, preferably Greek Metaxa

2 tablespoons clear honey

a round springform cake pan, 8 inches in diameter, lightly oiled and lined with parchment

SERVES 8–12

Halvas is a classic semolina and almond cake-like dessert. Greeks know its golden formula—1,2,3,4—by heart: 1 cup olive oil, 2 cups semolina, 3 cups sugar, and 4 cups water. This dessert can be elaborated into a proper baked cake like this one, using olive oil, not butter. Serve it with a blob of thick yogurt and a glass of Greek Metaxa brandy for a real treat.

Put the olive oil, sugar, and eggs in a large bowl and beat with an electric beater until light and fluffy. Reserve a handful of the walnut pieces for decoration and chop the remainder with a knife or food processor in brief bursts until fine, but not mealy.

Add to the bowl, together with the flour, salt, and yogurt. Using broad strokes, mix the batter with a wooden spoon until smooth and even. Do not overmix.

Spoon the mixture into the prepared cake pan and smooth flat on top. Scatter with the reserved nuts.

Bake towards the top of a preheated oven at 325°F for 40 minutes.

Test the center—a skewer inserted into the center should come out clean. Listen for a popping, bubbling sound too.

Put the brandy and honey in a small bowl and stir until dissolved. Trickle the mixture over the top of the cake, then let cool in the tin for 20 minutes.

Remove the cake, still on its metal base, and cool on a wire rack for 10 minutes. Remove the base, peel off the paper, and serve warm or cold. The cake will keep in an airtight container for 4 days.

This Mediterranean cake is packed with the flavors of Sicily with its hillsides of olive, orange, and lemon trees, almonds in baskets, and bottles of orange-flower water redolent of its Arab past. Instead of flour there is semolina and ground almonds; instead of butter, there is oil, and there are no dairy products whatsoever. Serve dusted with confectioners' sugar with a scoop of citrus sorbet. Alternatively, enjoy it purely as a cake with a tiny espresso and a glass of ice-cold water.

semolina citrus cake

Reserve a little of the shredded lemon and orange peel and put the remainder in a bowl with the olive oil, sugar, salt, orange and lemon juice, and eggs. Beat together with an electric beater or balloon whisk until well mixed and smooth.

Sieve the semolina and baking powder into a second bowl and add the ground almonds. Fold the almond extract and orange-flower water into the egg mixture. Pour all at once into the dry ingredients, fold together, but do not overmix. Spoon into the prepared cake pan and smooth the top.

Bake towards the top of a preheated oven at 325°F for 40–45 minutes or until pale gold at the edges and firm in the middle. A skewer inserted into the center should come out clean.

Remove from the oven and let cool in the pan for about 10 minutes. Drizzle the liqueur over the top. Push the cake out, still on its metal base, and let cool on a wire rack for another 10 minutes. Remove the base and peel off the paper. Serve in 8 or 12 wedges, warm or cool, but not chilled.

The cake will keep in an airtight container for up to 4 days.

shredded or grated peel and juice of 1 lemon

shredded or grated peel and juice of 1 orange

¾ cup extra virgin olive oil

1 cup sugar

¼ teaspoon salt

3 eggs

1½ cups semolina

1 cup ground almonds, tightly packed

1 teaspoon baking powder

1 teaspoon almond extract

1 teaspoon orange-flower water

4 tablespoons Cointreau or Grand Marnier

a round springform cake pan, 9 inches in diameter, lightly oiled and lined with parchment

SERVES 8–12

cinnamon toast with honey

⅔ cup milk

1 vanilla bean, split lengthwise

freshly grated peel of 1 lemon

3 large eggs, beaten

1 long baguette-style loaf, cut into 8 slices

¼ cup moscatel wine

olive oil, for frying

TO SERVE

⅓ cup clear honey

ground cinnamon, for dusting

5 sugar cubes, coarsely crushed, or 2 tablespoons regular sugar

SERVES 4–8

A more delicious version of French toast, torrija is one of Spain's best-loved treats. It is a sweet bread fritter that is eaten for dessert or in confiserías (cake shops) as a snack with a café cortado (coffee with a "cut" of milk). Easter is the big time for torrijas, but you find them all year round. In Spain, you would use the everyday pan de pueblo—a long loaf with a crisp crust—but a baguette will work fine.

Put the milk in a saucepan with the vanilla bean and lemon peel and heat to just below boiling point. Remove from the heat and let cool. When cool, beat in the eggs.

Strain the mixture into a flat dish large enough to take 2 slices of bread at a time. Put the slices of bread on a tray and sprinkle with the wine, just to moisten slightly.

Dip 2 slices of bread into the egg mixture and let soak for a few minutes. Heat the olive oil in a skillet over medium heat, add the soaked bread, and fry until golden brown on both sides, about 4 minutes. Drain on paper towels. Repeat until all are done.

Transfer to a large serving dish and spoon over the honey, sprinkle with cinnamon and sugar, and either let soak for a few hours or eat while hot.

If eating them cold, add the sugar just before serving.

a pinch of salt

finely grated peel of 1 lemon

1 teaspoon safflower oil,
plus extra for deep-frying

1 cup all-purpose flour, sifted

1 large egg, beaten with
1 tablespoon cold water

caster sugar, for dusting

CHOCOLATE A LA TAZA

8 oz. semisweet chocolate,
about 50% cocoa solids, broken
into squares

2 tablespoons sugar

a stick of cinnamon

2 tablespoons fine rice flour

an electric deep-fryer (optional)

*a strong pastry bag
fitted with a star tip*

a wide, oiled spatula

MAKES ABOUT 12: SERVES 4

After a night of revelry doing what Spaniards do best (eating, drinking, and talking), churros and hot chocolate at dawn are compulsory, ensuring a blissful sleep. A chocolate a la taza (cup of hot chocolate) for dunking churros must be thick—more like a sauce than a drink. The commercial chocolate made for this purpose has rice flour in it.

churros with hot chocolate

To make the churros, put 1 cup cold water in a medium saucepan with the salt, lemon peel, and oil. Bring to a fast boil, then add the flour all at once. Beat quickly with a wooden spoon to bring the mixture to a smooth paste, then leave for 5 minutes. Beat the egg mixture into the paste a little at a time until smooth and thick.

Fill a saucepan or deep-fryer one-third full with the oil, or to the manufacturer's recommended level. Heat to 375°F.

Working in batches if necessary, spoon the mixture into the pastry bag. Pipe horseshoe shapes onto the oiled spatula, cutting the flow of dough at 6-inch intervals with a knife or scissors. Slide them into the oil and fry for about 4 minutes until a rich gold, drain on paper towels and dust with sugar, heaping it on top as well, in true Spanish style.

To make the *chocolate a la taza*, put the chocolate, sugar, and 3⅔ cups cold water in a saucepan with the cinnamon stick and slowly melt the chocolate. Put the rice flour in small bowl, add 4 tablespoons cold water, and mix until smooth. Blend it into the chocolate, mix well, and bring just to a boil. If too thick, add a little water and reheat. Serve hot with the churros.

iced lemon crush

coarsely grated peel and freshly squeezed juice of 8 lemons

1 cup superfine sugar

crushed ice (optional)

SERVES 4

Put the lemon peel and sugar in a saucepan with 1 cup cold water and bring to a boil for 5 minutes. Strain. Add 2 cups cold water and the lemon juice, pour into a freezerproof container, and freeze for about 1 hour until ice crystals have formed around the edge. Break up with a fork and serve. Add extra crushed ice, if using.

Both of these drinks are perfect on baking hot days. Iced lemon crush is just a very simple lemonade. The Moorish version of horchata was made with pine nuts, seeds, and chufas or tiger nuts (which aren't nuts, but a tuberous root) and used as a "pick-me-up." Almonds can also be used instead of tiger nuts. The drink can be found freshly made in horchaterias and ice cream parlors, chilled and delicious.

horchata

2 cups blanched almonds, coarsely chopped

3 tablespoons sugar

freshly squeezed juice of 1 lemon

crushed ice, to serve (optional)

ground cinnamon, for dusting

SERVES 4

Put the almonds, sugar, and 1 cup water in a blender and grind as finely as possible. Pour into a pitcher or bowl and add 2¾ cups boiling water. Set aside to infuse for several hours until cold. Pour through a fine-mesh nylon strainer into a pitcher or bowl, pressing the liquid through with the back of a ladle. Stir in the lemon juice and pour into a freezerproof container.

Freeze for about 1 hour until crystals start to form. Stir well and serve in tall glasses with extra crushed ice, if using, and a dusting of cinnamon.

Mint tea is very soothing after a spicy meal. The sugar is traditionally added before the boiling water, but you may wish to serve it separately. Don't use spearmint as it will taste like mouthwash.

moroccan mint tea

Heat the teapot with just-boiled water. Tip out the water, add the tea leaves, and pour a little boiling water over them just to moisten. Swirl around, then quickly pour the water out again, taking care not to lose any leaves. Add a good handful of mint (add the sugar at this stage, if liked). Pour about 1 quart boiling water over the mint and moistened tea leaves. Put on the lid and leave to infuse for 5–8 minutes. Pour into warmed glasses and top with a few extra mint leaves. Hand the sugar around separately, if liked.

1½ heaping tablespoons green tea leaves

a handful of fresh mint leaves

about ¾ cup sugar, or to taste

SERVES 6

index

index

conversion charts

Weights and measures have been rounded up or down
slightly to make measuring easier.

Volume equivalents

American	Metric	Imperial
1 teaspoon	5 ml	
1 tablespoon	15 ml	
¼ cup	60 ml	2 fl.oz.
⅓ cup	75 ml	2½ fl.oz.
½ cup	125 ml	4 fl.oz.
⅔ cup	150 ml	5 fl.oz. (¼ pint)
¾ cup	175 ml	6 fl.oz.
1 cup	250 ml	8 fl.oz.

Weight equivalents   **Measurements**

Imperial	Metric	Inches	cm
1 oz.	25 g	¼ inch	5 mm
2 oz.	50 g	½ inch	1 cm
3 oz.	75 g	¾ inch	1.5 cm
4 oz.	125 g	1 inch	2.5 cm
5 oz.	150 g	2 inches	5 cm
6 oz.	175 g	3 inches	7 cm
7 oz.	200 g	4 inches	10 cm
8 oz. (½ lb.)	250 g	5 inches	12 cm
9 oz.	275 g	6 inches	15 cm
10 oz.	300 g	7 inches	18 cm
11 oz.	325 g	8 inches	20 cm
12 oz.	375 g	9 inches	23 cm
13 oz.	400 g	10 inches	25 cm
14 oz.	425 g	11 inches	28 cm
15 oz.	475 g	12 inches	30 cm
16 oz. (1 lb.)	500 g		
2 lb.	1 kg		

Oven temperatures

225°F	110°C	Gas ¼
250°F	120°C	Gas ½
275°F	140°C	Gas 1
300°F	150°C	Gas 2
325°F	160°C	Gas 3
350°F	180°C	Gas 4
375°F	190°C	Gas 5
400°F	200°C	Gas 6
425°F	220°C	Gas 7
450°F	230°C	Gas 8
475°F	240°C	Gas 9

credits

RECIPES

Clare Ferguson
Babaghannouj
Bell peppers stuffed with caperberries
Bitter chocolate and hazelnut gelato
Boeuf en daube
Bouillabaisse
Bresaola and arugula with olive oil and Parmesan
Caponata
Chicken liver and bacon
Chicken tagine with apricots
Chickpea fritters
Clams with chili parsley sauce
Classic lemon tart
Fougasse
Greek chicken stifado
Greek honey, walnut, and brandy cake
Linguine with pesto alla genovese
Luganega country sausage with lentils and wilted greens
Moroccan-style marinated black olives
Pappardelle with seafood sauce
Piperrada
Pork fillet with Marsala
Provençal roasted chicken with garlic, lemons, and olives
Provençal vegetable tian
Salade Niçoise
Sicilian schiacciata
Seafood with couscous
Semolina citrus cake
Sicilian spaghetti
Spaghetti alla carbonara
Spanish fishcakes
Spanish flans
Spanish roasted vegetables
Sugared strawberries

Linda Tubby
Artichokes provençal
Churros with hot chocolate

Cinnamon toast with honey
Cream of asparagus soup
Duck with olives
Garlic shrimp
Gazpacho
Hake in garlic sauce with clams
Horchata
Iced lemon crush
Lamb cutlets with salsa salmoretta
Mint and parsley salad
Pan-grilled steaks with olive sauce
Potato fritters with chorizo
Salad of belgian endive and blue cheese

Maxine Clark
Almond milk granita, laced with Amaretto
Braised sea bass with fennel and green olives
Caramelized fig tart
Cassoulet
Cauliflower with saffron and toasted bread crumbs
Egyptian dukkah
Fresh tuna carpaccio
Grilled mixed vegetable salad with balsamic herb dressing
Grilled sardines with salmoriglio sauce
Meat roll simmered in tomato sauce
Moroccan butterflied and grilled lamb
Moroccan mint tea
Moules marinière
Orange, frisée, and black olive salad
Paella
Panna cotta with candied orange peel
Pissaladière
Pizza alla margherita
Pizza rustica
Pork and fennel meatballs in tomato sauce
Ratatouille

Red mullet and orange packages
Rosemary focaccia
Sesame and mint couscous with winter vegetables
Sicilian green vegetables
Slow-roasted tomatoes on bruschetta with salted ricotta
Spinach with anchovies and pine nuts
Sweet and sour carrots and zucchini with mint
Three marinated antipasti
Tomato, mozzarella, and basil salad
Vanilla gelato with hot cherry sauce
Watermelon sorbet with chocolate chip seeds
White bean and black olive crostini
Whole onions baked in their skins

Elsa Petersen-Schepelern
Avgolemono
French duck salade tiède
Greek salad
Neopolitan seafood stew
Soupe au pistou
Tonno e fagioli
Warm chicken salad with harissa dressing

Fran Warde
Osso bucco with gremolata
Warm Mediterranean Puy lentil salad

Rena Salaman
Baked eggplants with garlic and tomatoes
Baked kibbeh
Falafel
Grilled tuna kabobs
Hoummus
Okra with dried limes
Spicy meat pastries
Spinach and cheese pie
Stuffed vine leaves

Jennie Shapter
Grilled bell pepper frittata

Brian Glover
Fish baked with lemon, oregano, and potatoes
Grilled fish with chermoula and grilled lemons

Silvana Franco
Pasta con le vongole

Louise Pickford
Souvlaki with bulghur wheat salad
Turkish pizza turnover

Sonia Stevenson
Roast gigot of monkfish with sauce Niçoise
Tuna with paprika crumbs and romesco sauce

PHOTOGRAPHS

KEY: a=above, b=below, r=right, l=left, c=center

Peter Cassidy
Pages 1, 3 all, 4l, 4-5, 7, 8al, 8ac, 8br, 11, 12, 15, 16, 21, 28, 31, 35, 39, 40, 44, 48al, 48br, 49, 55, 56, 67, 73, 74, 79, 80, 82bl, 92, 95, 102, 106, 112ar, 112bl, 112br, 113, 114, 117, 130, 145, 146, 148al, 148bl, 148br, 149, 150, 159, 160, 165, 166, 168, 171, 172, 175, 176, 178al, 178bl, 178br, 183, 185, 204br, 224, 227

Martin Brigdale
Pages 5r, 22, 32, 37, 43, 48ar, 51, 52, 58, 63, 64, 77, 82br, 90, 97, 101, 105, 109, 119,

120, 123, 129, 135, 136, 139, 143, 156, 163, 178ac, 178ar, 180, 189, 190, 193, 197, 199, 200, 206, 209, 211, 212, 214, 221, 222, 228, 231, 232

Noel Murphy
Pages 19, 83, 84, 89, 124, 132, 153, 155, 179, 194, 235

Debi Treloar
Pages 8bl, 69, 82al, 140, 148ar, 204ar, 204bl

Jan Baldwin
Pages 8ar, 82ar, 82bc, endpapers

Ian Wallace
Pages 112al, 127, 202, 204al

Jean Cazals
Pages 205, 217, 219

Gus Filgate
Pages 9, 25, 26

Diana Miller
Pages 48bl, 61, 70

Richard Jung
Pages 98, 111

Chris Tubbs
Pages 2, 6

Tara Fisher
Page 47

Jeremy Hopley
Page 87

Tom Leighton
Page 204ac

William Lingwood
Page 186